Highway to
HEALTH

Highway to
HEALTH

ANTIOXIDANTS & YOU
The food way to health and happiness

DR ROSS WALKER
Author of Best Sellers – 'If I Eat Another Carrot I'll Go Crazy'
and 'What's Cookin' Doc'

GOKO Management (ACN 002 530 298)

Level 8, 182-186 Blues Point Road

McMahons Point NSW 2060, Australia

Phone: (02) 9922 5334   Fax: (02) 9922 5343

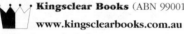

Kingsclear Books (ABN 99001904034)

www.kingsclearbooks.com.au

P.O. Box 335 Alexandria 1435

Phone (02) 9439 5093   Fax (02) 9439 0430

ISBN 0-908272-62-6

First printed 2000

Front cover design by New Frontier

Illustrations by Dennis Richards

Printed by Griffin Press

CONTENTS

※

Dedicated to:
Paul, Alexandra, David,
Bridget & Isabelle

INTRODUCTION

As a doctor and cardiologist I have spent many years treating disease but over the past five years have focused on prevention. Many doctors offer lip service to prevention. They do not put much effort into developing plans, programs or preventative strategies for their patients, or for that matter, for themselves.

If you want to stay healthy, you need a plan. How long do you plan to live? I didn't ask, 'When do you plan to die?' I want you to think about real quality of life as well as quantity. Are you planning to go out in your sixties, or your seventies or even higher? Do you have a plan for optimum health?

I want to live until I am one hundred. Not because I'm afraid of death, but because I love life. I don't want to spend my last 20 to 30 years battling heart disease, cancer or arthritis. Basically I want to enjoy the same good health I enjoy at present.

Every day in my busy cardiology practice I am asked questions by my patients. Many of the questions relate to how they can achieve better health. When I speak on health topics I am constantly approached by people who, for personal use and in many cases business reasons, want to know more about nutrition, antioxidants, health assessments and other health issues. I have tried to answer most of these questions in this book and provide a plan for your optimum health.

I must point out that I see nutritional supplementation as an addition to standard medical therapy. Standard medical therapy has a proven, scientific track record and has saved many lives. Don't ever regard any type of supplementation as a replacement for healthy lifestyle, appropriate medical assessments and proven medical therapies. As with all advice given in books or journals, it is important to discuss your symptoms, your condition and your treatment with your family doctor.

CHAPTER ONE

HIGHWAY TO HEALTH

Kevin Arnold is 62 years old. He is thin and has lived, what his friends and doctors would consider an excellent lifestyle. Despite this, Kevin began experiencing chest pain when he exercised or if he became upset. He was referred to me for a stress echo procedure (a sophisticated form of exercise testing that shows how the heart performs under load). His results were abnormal, suggesting blockages in his coronary arteries. This is the usual precursor to heart attack. A coronary angiogram (dye study of the coronary arteries) was performed which showed moderate blockages in his arteries. The results were bad enough to justify his symptoms and test results but not severe enough to justify an operation or other invasive treatment.

Kevin commenced a program of lifestyle modification, aggressive cholesterol lowering and antioxidant treatment. Within three months, Kevin's chest pain had disappeared and a repeat stress echo 12 months later was normal.

Over the past ten years new medical evidence has emerged that heart disease can be controlled and, in some cases, with appropriate treatment, be reversed. Evidence is also emerging that antioxidant therapy is gaining increasing importance as an integral part of this treatment.

Many members of the medical profession do not support the use of antioxidants, especially in people without any obvious disease. An interesting statistic from America revealed 50% of cardiologists took antioxidant dose vitamins but only 30% prescribed them for their patients. This sounds horribly like hedging your bets both ways. As I will show you in this book, the scientific and medical evidence in support of vitamins is increasing. Unfortunately the conservative elements in the medical profession feel we should all wait for long term scientific trials before across–the–board recommendations to people about preventative vitamin consumption are made.

As I will demonstrate later, proper trials of antioxidant dose vitamins in healthy people over a reasonable time period will never be done. To date there have been a number of trials performed, most on either smokers or people who were initially malnourished, and all for less than ten years. There are many good reasons why these trials were doomed to failure from the outset and it is for this reason I believe they should be disregarded.

I must state that I believe antioxidant dose vitamins are no substitute for a healthy diet and lifestyle. We now live in a society that is geared for comfort. From push button entertainment to pills for almost every ailment. We basically think we have it all. The problem is that these simple answers are usually Band–Aid solutions to a much deeper problem. The lack of commitment in our society to ongoing healthy lifestyle principles, and the desire to follow many and varied unhealthy practices, contributes to our growing health (or should I say disease) bill. So, although I am a great advocate of antioxidants, I will state emphatically from the outset that they are of limited value unless used in conjunction with a healthy lifestyle.

In America 50% of cardiologists take antioxidant dose vitamins but only 30% prescribe them for their patients.

A healthy lifestyle does not mean becoming a disciple to Nathan Pritikin, running the Boston Marathon or attending regular yoga classes. A healthy lifestyle is not a rigorous, draconian almost monastic existence. These perceptions of lifestyle change make following such principles unacceptable and unachievable for most people, apart from those you would assiduously avoid at a cocktail party. Mind you, such people are easy to pick. They're the ones drinking water and chewing a celery stick with that 'well at least my coronary arteries are whistle clean' look on their smiling self satisfied faces.

In reality these people are deluding themselves into believing they're healthier than the rest of us. The delusion they live under is that 'boring deprivation' affords a health benefit. It doesn't!

The true health benefit comes from following what the Buddhists call the 'middle path' that is moderation in all aspects of life.

Here are five key areas that you need to consider as you start your optimum health plan.

1. Diet
2. Exercise
3. Smoking
4. Alcohol
5. Stress

Diet

The evidence is now overwhelming that a long term Mediterranean diet allows the greatest protection from our two biggest killers – heart disease and cancer.

The closer we are to vegetarian, the longer we live. Most studies support vegetarianism as a pathway to excellent health. It is suggested that vegetarians live seven years longer than the rest of us (although the more committed carnivores amongst us say it just feels like seven years). Vegetarians have 30% less heart disease than meat eaters. The combination of red meat, minimal nut and legume intake and increased body weight increases your bowel cancer risk by around four times.

A recent study from Lyon in France, performed on 600 Frenchmen following a heart attack, showed a 75% reduction (over a two year period) in heart disease and other mortality in the 300 Frenchmen placed on the Mediterranean diet, compared with the others on a standard low fat diet.

Now, four years on in the study, the benefit remains for

those who have maintained the eating plan. Let's face it, it's not difficult to follow a 'diet' that involves pastas and rice, extra virgin olive oil, nuts, legumes, fruits and vegetables washed down with two glasses of nature's finest antioxidant, red wine.

Basically as far as food goes, we don't have to maintain a boring, low fat diet to achieve good health. There is not a shred of scientific evidence to support the use of a standard low fat diet (20 to 25% of daily energy in fat) as a means to maintain health, prevent heart disease or prevent cancer.

So why bother? One of the reasons given is to keep your weight down. But, I am not suggesting you should swim in olive oil and eat packet after packet of salted roasted nuts – it's about consuming foods in moderation.

A study by Professor Ancel Keys, known as the Seven Countries Study (which you may be shocked to find studied seven countries!) found the people of Crete had the lowest rates of heart disease, even lower than the Japanese. In fact, the heart disease rate in Finland was 30 times higher than Crete. In the region in Crete studied, there were only two heart attacks in the first five years and one was the local town butcher.

The Mediterranean diet includes olive oil, pasta, rice, cheese, leafy greens, tomatoes, red peppers, dried beans and peas, nuts, fresh fruit and a little red wine.

The people of Crete live for ten to 15 years longer than the rest of us. They have little heart disease, cancer and diabetes, despite the fact that their basic diet is around 40% fat. Someone should let the villagers of Crete know that their normal way of eating is part of ongoing scientific nutritional evidence for the benefits of a Mediterranean diet. Most likely they wouldn't care because they already find their lifestyle most satisfying.

Exercise

What about exercise? Do we really need to pound the pavement or don the leotards and get off to our aerobic classes at the gym? Well, the answer is yes, if you want to, but the reality is we need around half an hour of exercise, four to five times per week.

Just as important as exercise is a little concept you may not have heard of known as movement. Yes, you are allowed to move. Try it right now. Take those two things below your hips and stand up and walk. Try to see everything you do every day as an opportunity for movement. Take the stairs rather than the escalators. Park further away from your destination and walk the rest of the way.

Good fats include olive oil, canola oil and avocados. These are monounsaturated. The bad fats in meat and butter are saturated fats.

Smoking

Don't smoke. Need I say anymore?

Alcohol

If you have never had a problem with alcohol in the past, consuming one to two glasses of red wine per day does have a significant health benefit. Remember, you don't get double the benefit with double the dose!

Stress

I believe we should all have around half an hour per day when we practice some technique that cranks our brain down to nothing. Something that rids us of all those extraneous thoughts that plague us throughout the day. This should be in addition to sleep. What I am suggesting is one of the following:

1. Meditation – this is the form of release I use. The health and life benefits of regular meditation are enormous. One long term study showed a 50 to 60% reduction in heart disease and cancer by the simple practice of daily meditation.
2. Relaxation therapy – although this is very useful, does not require the same discipline as meditation. Breathing techniques and progressive muscular relaxation are more popular. There are many excellent relaxation tapes available which can certainly assist the process.
3. Meditative prayer – for people with a strong religious belief, daily prayer is not only a vital time for communication with your Creator, but it is also a wonderful form of quiet time.
4. Sitting quietly enjoying a view.
5. A practice such as yoga.

High amounts of antioxidants in the blood stream can lessen free radical damage incurred during heavy exercise.

There are many other methods for clearing the mind and the best method is the one which you will perform on a daily basis.

If you follow these lifestyle principles, get regular medical assessments, eat antioxidants, drink purified water and have a purpose in your life, you will find that extra quantity and, probably even more importantly quality of life, that is optimum health.

CHAPTER TWO

QUALITY OF LIFE

Over the past ten years we have been bombarded with the phrase quality of life. Fifty years ago people were happy to survive. Our society is geared for comfort. We have 'push button' everything, including ordering items over the internet that are then delivered to our door.

With the way technology has been going, we could basically spend our lives sitting in a chair that could recline (automatically of course) to be a bed at night. We could live our lives giving voice commands to a computer that would also function as a television, radio, microwave and most other electrical appliances you can imagine. With a few minor modifications, it could also back up as a toilet, avoiding the need for any major movement!

We must realise that this quest for quality of life has been paralleled with an increasing lack of the need to move. Lack of movement does not really improve our quality of life, and in fact, goes a long way to harming this long term quest.

This quest for quality of life has been paralleled with an increasing lack of the need to move.

Our bodies were initially designed for movement and if we don't keep moving we run the risk of our moving parts seizing up. We all know the feeling when we first try to stand up and move after sitting in the one place for too long. That stiffness, especially in your knees and lower back, must be a sign that lack of movement is not without its consequences.

Quality of life

We need to seek quality and richness in all aspects of our existence. There are five additional quality areas we should be working on:

1. Quality of health
2. Quality of relationships and emotions
3. Quality of leisure
4. Quality of financial situation
5. Quality of spiritual life

Without work and effort in all five areas we cannot achieve true happiness and therefore true quality of life. Although some of these areas are more important than others, we need a balance in all of these aspects to achieve true quality of life.

Quality of health

My main purpose in writing this book is to offer you the key principles which will allow you to achieve optimum health. Although the main thrust of this book is the place of antioxidant and nutritional supplementation in the overall picture of optimum health, it is important from the outset that I stress that no supplement can be viewed as a replacement for a healthy lifestyle. A healthy lifestyle is more important as a key to life quality than any supplement, pharmaceutical drug, surgical procedure or medical intervention.

The five–point way to a healthy life (detailed in *If I eat another carrot, I'll go crazy*) is the start on the road that leads to optimum health.

1. Follow the correct dietary principles consistent with the Mediterranean diet
2. Continue a regular exercise and movement program
3. Don't smoke
4. If you have never had a problem with alcohol, consume 1–2 standard glasses (125 ml glass) of red wine per day
5. Practice a daily stress management technique

Regular walking or swimming will decrease your chances of degenerative diseases such as diabetes.

Quality of relationships and emotions

Quality of life is centred on our relationships and emotions. Part of our reason for existence is to nurture and care for those who are special to us. Any contribution to the lives of our loved ones will greatly enhance our own quality of life. At a purely physical level, having strong emotional support greatly enhances our longevity and reduces our risk of falling victim to one of the many common diseases. For example, in one study of women with breast cancer, survival was doubled in the group with strong emotional support.

Recent work showed a group of heart attack survivors, with a depressive illness, had twice the complication rates of those without depression. Clinical trials aside, there is no doubt when we are stressed, overworked or plain run down, we are much more prone to catching viral infections. From common simple infections to serious illnesses, if you know there is someone special around who cares about you, you have a much better chance of a rapid recovery.

At home we have what my father–in–law calls the 'healing lounge'. In fact, I doubt this lounge is all that unique to the Walker household. As soon as any member of my family feels unwell, you can see them

When we are stressed we are prone to catching viruses.

sprawled out on the lounge in front of the television. And sure enough, within a few days they're perfectly well. That lounge sure has magical healing properties. I am certainly not suggesting that the extra TLC from my wife does not contribute to the lounge's healing properties. Strangely enough, she hardly ever gets sick enough to occupy the healing lounge — something odd about mothers.

How many people (especially men) lose their emotional balance? In the corporate world people are so driven by their companies to 'give their all' to the organisation. Your performance is judged by productivity and, unfortunately, how many hours you stay at work.

Barry Seymour is 44 years old. He was married at 31 and now has two children, a nine year old boy and a five year old girl. Barry works as a financial manager in a large consulting firm and is well respected in this very competitive industry. He lives in the north western region of Sydney, Australia, and the trip by car into central Sydney can take up to an hour each way. He leaves at 6.00 am and usually arrives home exhausted anywhere between 7.30 pm and 9.00 pm.

If he's lucky, he may spend ten minutes with his children but he is usually too tired to read with them and hardly ever has an evening meal with his family. His wife (understandably) is becoming increasingly disgruntled with his time away from home, especially seeing he is often away weekends at conferences, or playing golf with important clients. A few years before, he was the coach of his son's soccer team. Now he would be lucky to make it to any of the games.

When Barry is asked why he is spending so much time away from the family, he gives the standard answer we hear so often, 'If I really put the effort in now, my family will have enormous benefits later on'. Although this sounds like a reasonable answer, nothing could be further from the truth. The real benefit to any family is time, not just 'quality time' but plain old 'time' itself. These people say, 'I really put a big effort into those ten minutes I spend with my kids everyday'. They must be kidding! Eventually when Barry has the necessary time to spend with his family, they will be adults and not have enough time for him. If he's lucky, his wife may tolerate his absence from home. Often this scenario precipitates a wife seeking her emotional needs elsewhere. It's all about balance, Barry.

Quality of leisure

The third aspect is quality of leisure. We can't put all our eggs in the 'work' or 'home' basket. It is important to have some leisure activities such as sport, music or other hobbies that round us out as human beings.

Leisure activity, however, should be a joy and not a chore. I play competition soccer and often some of the players think they are playing the World Cup. It's basically just a kick around on a Saturday afternoon for a group of over 35 year old 'geriatrics' reliving past glories. It's also basically a pretty good way of maintaining fitness. However, for some people who play relatively high–level competition sport, the carry on over line calls or rulings and the heated arguments that follow, are amazing. It's bad enough when world ranked players make spectacles of themselves, but when there is definitely no match prize money, why bother? Just enjoy.

Quality of financial situation

The quality of our financial situation should not be disregarded. We all have to survive in a competitive, stressful world and often this takes enormous personal exertion. Most of us dream of being independently wealthy, owning a business that does not require ongoing personal effort.

People in professional jobs know only too well that the only money they make is the money earned from their direct face to face contact with clients.

I know myself as a medical doctor, if I take a week off, I earn no money but still have to pay the staff and the leases on my equipment, not to mention the rent. Work is one important basis for self–esteem, but the constant pressure to produce cash flow does detract from the enjoyment of the job.

The stress of financial hardship is enormous. This is one of the greatest pressures on a family and it is important that intelligent, motivated people are always seeking excellent business opportunities. Another important aspect of work is that you enjoy what you do. It doesn't matter how much financial success you have, unless you enjoy it, you will eventually lose out.

We enjoy our work for many different reasons. We all have different personalities and different motivations. It is vital you understand your own

Stress can create muscular tension, shallow breathing, rapid heart rate and over time contribute to a weakened immune system.

reasons for what attracts you to a particular kind of work. Income is not the only reason. Some people enjoy direct contact with other people, while others enjoy working alone. Some enjoy the best of both worlds.

It is interesting if you look, for example, at artists, where some enjoy the act of painting as a form of meditation or relaxation. Others enjoy the personal satisfaction of the finished product or purely enjoy their own creation. Others, however, enjoy the accolades they may achieve from those who admire their work. The example can extend to any form of work, and although we all strive to produce excellent results, it can be seen how different our motives are. Whatever your motivation, you will find it hard to sustain a quality financial situation without enjoyment of your work.

Quality of the spiritual

The fifth and probably the most important, is the quality of our spiritual lives. What are your deeper life goals? In fact, have you ever considered this question? We spend so much of our lives in what Yeats calls the 'daily trivial mind'. Our focus is on issues that are often important at the time (our enjoyment of a meal, what time the next train leaves, what television show will we watch) but in the grand scheme of things will have no bearing on our spiritual development.

Balance in all aspects of your life is the key. Without balance there is no quality.

Our beliefs direct our value system. Do you have a reason to exist? Do you know that your growth as a total human being is furthered by service to others? Mother Theresa was one of the greatest people of the twentieth century. Her greatness came from her enormous commitment to service. This service was to assist destitute people who are often shunned by most members of society. We revere people like Mother Theresa, and I often wonder whether some of that reverence is because when we see and hear of the extraordinary service given by such a person, it reflects our desire to act in a similar fashion.

It is important to realise that our earth is functioning through one major motivating force. This force is not the desire for power over others, the desire for wealth, or the desire for possessions.   No, the major motivating force is love. We all need to be loved but, more importantly, we all need to love.

We all need to be loved but, more importantly, we all need to love.

Rare people like Mother Theresa have this enormous capacity for universal, unconditional love. We can all have this same capacity. Like Mother Theresa, we should manifest this love through unconditional service to others.

If you can rid yourself of the concept of 'I'm doing this because it will benefit me in some way', and truly perform whatever act you want to perform purely for the other person's benefit, then your own personal power will increase enormously.

Steven Covey states in his superb book, *The Seven Habits of Highly Successful People*, that many of us are climbing the ladder to success only to find we have the ladder leaning against the wrong wall.

The wrong wall is always the wall of personal benefit. There is absolutely no problem with earning money, receiving accolades or the respect of others or even driving around in a luxury car, but if these are your major motivations you will never achieve satisfaction and never have true quality of life.

True quality of life comes from achieving a balance in health, relationships, emotions, leisure, finance and your spiritual self.

True quality of life comes from achieving a balance in all five aspects of your life. Your health, your relationships and emotions, your leisure, your financial situation and your spiritual self. With an imbalance or the wrong motivations in any of these areas quality of life is eroded.

CHAPTER THREE

LONGEVITY
IS IT JUST LUCK?

Most people, when they hear the angel of death flapping around their ears, would like a bit more time, if the truth be known, a lot more time! Fear of the unknown is strong motivation to stay well and keep sucking in as much oxygen as your lungs will allow. As Woody Allen put it, 'It's not that I'm afraid of death, I just don't want to be there when it happens?' Death has such a final ring to it. My attitude is, 'Let's do everything we can to put off the inevitable'.

Is longevity just pure good luck or are there other controllable factors that contribute to us surviving well past the biblical concept of three score and ten? It is your genetics that load the gun and your environment that pulls the trigger?

There is no doubt that there are some people who are born with the genetic short straw. Alternatively, there are people, no matter what piece of Western poison they indulge in (saturated fat, cigarette smoke, refined sugars and alcohol) who will survive into their eighties and nineties. These people, at either end of the spectrum, are few in number. Most of us fit into the category where our genetics and our environment play equal roles in the generation of illnesses and our eventual demise.

Malcolm Seaton was 28. He was a high flyer in every sense of the word. Despite his young age, he was a partner in a growing software company. He enjoyed the 'good life'. Although he was thin, he did not watch his diet, smoked cigarettes, drank too much and played hard. He was single and was often seen at the chic places around town with a different gorgeous woman on his arm each night of the week. He loved to ski and would often travel overseas to engage in his passion. During a particularly strenuous session in Aspen, Colorado, he collapsed on the slopes and could not be resuscitated.

Why did Malcolm die so early? His fast lane existence didn't help but let's face it, there are many people in his age group where this behaviour is the norm and, despite burning the candle at both ends, still manage to survive. The reason for Malcolm's premature exit was his poor genetics. Malcolm had a condition known as familial hypercholesterolaemia. Fifty percent of sufferers of this condition have a major vascular event before the age of 50. It is obvious that we need early detection for these people with bad genetics. We also need to use whatever tricks we have available to us to treat them.

Is there a secret of eternal youth, which will promote longevity? Good genetics is an excellent starting point but is not an absolute guarantee for a long life. It is hard to compare each generation. We must remember our ancestors survived in a different age and their environment was far removed from anything we know today. Their stress, their foods, even their air was different. Don't say, 'Dad and mum are both alive in their eighties and dad smoked, therefore, I'll keep smoking and I'll be right'. Having longevity in your family should make you more intent on living the right lifestyle, rather than destroying yourself.

HAD THE THERAPEUTIC BENEFITS
OF BISON-EXTRACT BEEN OVERSTATED?
BERYL AND GERT DECIDED TO INVESTIGATE.

Having a long life is not found in the miracle cures that you see advertised on TV. Consider Jean Goodman who is 53. We are told that she has been battling arthritis for the last four years. Within three days of starting 'Jointex', her joint swelling was settling and her pain had gone. Whereas before she was stiff in her joints in the morning for an hour, this now only lasts for approximately five minutes. 'Jointex' is a purely natural product taken from the gall bladder of a bison. Bisons have never been known to suffer joint pain that they specifically complained about to a doctor. Often these arguments are about as scientific as it gets, and people still flock to purchase the product.

Although a 'natural cure' for anything is very appealing, it hardly ever works. If I can give you a 'sugar pill' or placebo for any condition and assure you it works, there is a 40% chance it will work. One should never discount the power of the mind. People who have more confidence in their doctors have faster healing rates and a much greater chance of a cure than those who lack respect for their doctors or do not believe in their treatment. I am not suggesting that all natural cures do not work. Please be cautious when you are told that one particular treatment is a 'cure all' because it almost certainly is not.

You hear the myth about people living in small pockets of the earth who live to the age of 130 to 140 and are very healthy throughout their life. Over the age of 100 they are still riding horseback, swimming in cold streams and making love without the use of Viagra.

'Please give me what they're taking,' you may say. Do these people have a real magic to their lives? Is there some wondrous formula that prevents serious aging? The answer to all these questions is yes!

Time is variable for all of us. Time in the dentist's chair may seem like an eternity. Living in the Hunza Valley in Pakistan, or areas of Georgia is pretty damn routine. Some would say boring. They break the monotony with birthday parties. So a man who says he is 110 years old and looks 50 to 60 is having five to six birthdays per year. So the secret to eternal youth is to have more birthday parties.

The oldest recorded life span (with a verified birth certificate) is a lady in France who died last century at the age of 122, having made a rap song the year before her death. The Guinness Book of Records reports a man in China who allegedly lived to around 250. He, of course, could not produce a birth certificate.

oh yeah...I'm a hunerd an twenny-three....
and my son's ninety-five next moon!

At the turn of the last century, the average life expectancy was around 50 years for men and women. Today this has skyrocketed to the mid–to–late seventies for men and the early eighties for women, depending on which race of people you survey.

The developing countries still have much lower life expectancies. The rates of different types of diseases also vary from place to place. Eastern Europeans have the highest heart disease rates in the world, whereas people who live the Mediterranean lifestyle, such as the residents of Crete, or those on a naturally low saturated fat diet such as Japan or rural China, have low rates of heart disease.

Developing countries are still plagued by many and varied infectious diseases. Despite better control in Western countries, HIV AIDS is devastating many African nations.

Cancer in its many forms is much more common in developed countries. Lung, breast, bowel and prostate cancer are the big killers. Each has their own particular associations but all have strong dietary links. For

The average life expectancy in Western society has increased to around 80 years.

example, although lung cancer is directly linked to cigarette smoke, people who have a diet high in saturated fat and who smoke have much higher rates of lung cancer than those who smoke and do not consume as much saturated fat. I am not advocating smokers should have a low saturated fat diet. I am suggesting both aspects of lifestyle are bad for you. You should not eat too much saturated fat and you should not smoke.

Luigi was a patient of mine. He strode into my office with a beaming smile, stating he was here for a check–up. As the conversation progressed, my eyes drifted to his file which revealed his birth date. Luigi was 91 years old. 'There must be some mistake', I said to him very surprised after this unexpected finding. 'Mistake about what?' he asked. 'Your age,' I replied. 'You couldn't possibly be 91?' He said, 'I am, I'll bring in my birth certificate to prove it if you like'.

'What's your secret, Luigi?' I asked, incredulously. He leaned forward and said with a twinkle in his eye, 'Doctor, you've got to have a passion.' 'What's your passion, Luigi?' I asked. His answer was almost as much a surprise as his age. 'My passion is orchids. I've won 2000 awards and 13 world gold medals for my orchids,' he proudly stated. I checked Luigi's heart and he was as strong as an ox. I congratulated him and he left.

Twelve months later he returned for another appointment. 'Luigi,' I said, 'You don't know how many people I've told about your 2000 awards and your 13 world gold medals'. He looked at me with amusement and said, 'Doctor, 14!'

This remarkable man, now 92 years old, ignored the fact that he should behave like an old man. He disregarded the fact that he had a 92 year old body. Luigi had a passion and lived his life to the fullest. His young wife of 73 found it hard to keep up with this amazing character. He will probably continue to win gold medals for his orchids until he decides he has had enough of life.

Luigi is what Wayne Dyer calls a 'no limit' person. Once you believe you have limits, once you accept the common view of life, once you decide to 'go along with the crowd', 'be a good compliant member of the tribe', 'be a subscriber to mediocrity' then guess what, you will become all those things. You'll retire when you're expected to, you'll have your major life illness at the appropriate time and then die on cue around your three score years and ten, possibly even before.

If, however, you don't find this 'crowd mentality' too appealing, you can always decide to do things differently. Your new life plan can be decided on and then you can start living the program. Part of that life plan must be your health plan. This plan should be simple, achievable and most importantly, enjoyable.

So what is the essence of longevity? The essence is to achieve balance in all aspects of your life. There are similar characteristics seen in almost all healthy octogenarians and nonagenarians:

1. They have good genetics
2. They eat a low saturated fat diet
3. They do not smoke
4. They have an independent outlook
5. Finally they all have a passion

CHAPTER FOUR

REGULAR MEDICAL ASSESSMENTS

Unfortunately many of us are walking around with a genetic time bomb in our body waiting to explode. In my field, cardiology, we can 'guess' who is most likely to have a vascular event (such as heart attack, angina or stroke) by looking at some simple parameters called risk factors.

There are five major risk factors and five minor risk factors for vascular disease.

Major risk factors

1. High cholesterol
2. Cigarette smoking
3. Hypertension (high blood pressure)
4. Diabetes
5. Family history of vascular disease before 55

Minor risk factors

1. Obesity
2. Physical inactivity
3. Stress
4. Specific infections
5. Gout

It is very important to note that if you have any of these factors, it does not automatically mean you will have a heart attack, angina or stroke. Also, if you do not have any of these factors, it does not mean you have no chance of developing any of these conditions. Basically if you have any of these major or a few of the minor risk factors, then you are at a higher risk. If these factors are absent, then you are at a lower risk.

To give you an example, if your cholesterol is elevated you have a three times higher risk for a heart attack than if your cholesterol is normal. Around 35% of people with heart attacks still have normal cholesterol levels.

The underlying cause of vascular disease is a process known as atherosclerosis which is a narrowing and hardening of the arteries. Every person who lives in Western society will develop some degree of atherosclerosis as they grow older.

If autopsies are performed on people who have died below the age of 30, for non–cardiac reasons, approximately 80% have already some degree of fat build–up in their arteries. Twenty percent of these people already have 50% or greater blockages.

The problem for cardiologists is sorting out who in our society will go on to develop the complications of this fat build up (such as heart attack, angina or stroke). There are many people in their eighties who are nervously watching their elevated cholesterol results, hoping for some salvation from this dreadful curse. These are the people who, despite having a major risk factor for vascular disease, will probably not develop marked disease. Why does this occur? No one really knows but it is felt to be due to the presence of other unknown protective factors in the body.

Saturated fat in the Western diet is associated with increased risk of cancer, diabetes and heart disease.

There are around 100,000 genes in the body determining anything from eye colour to how fast your heart beats. There are also genes that predispose you to clot formation and other genes that help break down clots. It really depends on which side your genes lean as to how much these risk factors will affect you.

For example, a study completed during the last decade of the twentieth century known as the West of Scotland Coronary Prevention Study followed 6,500 middle–aged men, all with raised cholesterol levels, over a five year period. Half were given a cholesterol–lowering drug (one of the powerful group of drugs known as the statins) and the other took a sugar pill (placebo).

Apart from their high cholesterol, these men had no prior history of heart disease. At the end of the study it was found that those who took the statin had a 30% reduction in their risk of heart disease and a 24% reduction in their risk of death from any causes.

The interesting statistic is that in reality, those with only high cholesterol as the single risk factor had around a 4% chance of any type of heart attack over a five year period. Those with multiple risk factors had a 10% risk for a heart attack over five years.

Let's take the optimist's view here. This means that with a high cholesterol and a combination of other risk factors such as cigarette smoking, high blood pressure, or a strong family history, you will have a 90% chance of not having a heart attack over the next five years.

I personally would be doing everything I could to minimise this risk but it still puts into perspective that just having a high cholesterol does not make you a walking time bomb. This is strengthened by the fact that you have a greater than 95% chance of surviving five years without a heart attack if your only problem is a high cholesterol.

Atherosclerosis is a fatty build up in the arteries. This can affect the arteries that supply the brain as well as the heart.

If you have stable heart disease (and don't follow my five point regression plan), you have a 2% chance of dying per year. Therefore over a 20 year period you have a 60% chance of being alive. Compare this to having high cholesterol alone but no obvious vascular disease. Over 20 years your risk for a heart attack (not death) should be around 20%. You have an 80% chance of not having a heart attack.

From this you can see, we are just talking statistics and also only one (or at most a few) factors at work in your life. We haven't even started to mention factors like your happiness, your relationships, your personal drive, your spiritual beliefs or your levels of anxiety. These factors are so much harder to quantify. Medical science loves numbers. A cholesterol level is a number that is measurable and reproducible. Emotional and psychological factors are difficult to measure and impossible to reproduce.

Antioxidants prevent cholesterol being oxidised and attaching to the artery wall.

Any medical assessment must be seen as a 'best guess'. Medical science is always striving for better answers and more accurate methods of assessment. However, I do not believe you should abandon medicine and I would strongly suggest that once you have reached 40 years of age, regular medical assessment should begin (unless you have a strong family history of premature heart disease or cancer then assessments should begin earlier).

So, you are now 40 and feel it is time for a check–up. Well, what is a check–up and are they all the same? What are the real benefits?

Firstly, a check–up is a vague term. It can range from a few questions, a few simple blood pathology tests along with a check of your blood pressure, all the way through to an intense, expensive work up that evaluates every aspect of preventative health.

Many people question the value of these expensive evaluations, arguing that most people who undergo such evaluations are at low risk anyhow, and therefore the cost of such assessments to find those at high risk, does not justify the expense. At a community or government level, I completely agree. It is not my position that the top end of the assessment trail should be subsidised by the government.

I believe that preventative health assessments should be the responsibility of the individual or their corporation. You may be stunned to realise that in Australia alone it costs big business around one billion dollars per year to replace executives culled by heart disease and cancer. The cost of life easily justifies the expense for any corporation.

At a personal level, although the yield of high tech screening programs for detecting otherwise unknown life–threatening disease is relatively low, there are otherwise numerous benefits to the individual. The sooner potential heart disease or cancer are detected, the more effective are preventative programs to either halt or reverse the disease.

It depends whether you want the budget assessment or the five star assessment with all the bells and whistles. It all comes down to cost and what a person is prepared to pay for their assessment. We move from the less expensive standard check up to the full medical overhaul and examine the pros and cons.

You walk into your family physician and ask for a basic check–up. A good doctor in this case will probably perform the following assessment.

Basic history

◆ Present symptoms – for example chest pain, shortness of breath, cough, change in bowel habit, urinary symptoms, vaginal bleeding, breast lump and so on, depending on whether you are male or female

◆ Risk factor profile – covering such items as history of cholesterol abnormalities, high blood pressure, cigarette smoking, alcohol consumption and other physical and behavioural factors

◆ Past medical history – covering items such as heart disease, prior cancer and operations

◆ Family medical history – including specific diseases and the ages they occurred, such as a heart attack in a father at 45 years old is of more concern than prostate cancer in an 88 year old uncle

◆ Social, medication and supplement history

Examinations

◆ Blood pressure, stethoscope to heart and lungs, abdominal and rectal examination, breast check and Pap smear

◆ Other tests such as ECG, prostate examination (males), mammography (females)

◆ Blood tests such as cholesterol, triglycerides, (HDL cholesterol), blood sugar, uric acid, PSA (males)

Your doctor may also perform what is known in some circles as an MBA 20. This is basically a general blood screen looking at electrolytes, kidney and liver function along with a few other tests. Simple urine analysis should also be performed.

These simple, inexpensive, screening procedures may detect the occasional person with an otherwise undiagnosed problem but are really not particularly effective at detecting early disease.

For example, a high cholesterol level only tells you your cholesterol level is high. It does not automatically mean you have a heart problem or even atherosclerosis (the fat build up in the lining of your arteries, which is the initial problem before you go on to develop heart disease).

Biochemical and physiological tests can detect early signs of disease. If you are over 50 an annual check–up is recommended.

The next level of assessment is the so–called Executive Health Check. This usually takes a few hours of your time and involves completing detailed questionnaires, a full physical examination and blood and urine tests similar to those performed in the basic check–up.

The Executive Health Check usually also involves an exercise test. As a screening test for heart disease, however, this is quite poor. If you line up 100 people with heart disease and perform a stress test, you will fail to diagnose the problem in around 30 people. If you then line up 100 healthy people without heart disease and perform the same test, you will find abnormalities in again around 30 people.

Therefore, the sensitivity (false negative rate in people with disease) is unacceptable as a screening test. This is, of course, different in people with definite exertion–based symptoms where stress testing is a more effective test. It is therefore, my opinion that stress testing should not be used as a screen for heart disease but is of value in determining the level of fitness. A much more sensitive and specific test is to combine imaging (either nuclear or echocardiography) with stress testing, where exercise stress testing alone requires around a 70% block in an artery to be positive, combining imaging with exercise usually detects around 50% or greater blockages. This is a much better test, but still misses the larger plaques that are in the wall of the artery that have not as yet ruptured to cause a heart attack, unstable angina or sudden cardiac death.

Around 70% of heart attacks occur in blockages that were less than 50% in size in the preceding six months. It is important to realise that although the blockages are minimal, the fatty plaque itself is quite large.

As fat builds up in the wall (a process that commences in the teens and early childhood), the actual channel where the blood flows still remains quite open.

At this stage a blockage of any importance will not be detected on an angiogram, despite the presence of a large plaque in the wall. The only non–invasive test than can detect these types of plaques (which I have just stated are the plaques that usually rupture) is the high speed gated coronary CT scan (HSGCCT).

I also believe it is important to have more advanced blood tests looking for Lp(a), homocysteine and apolipoprotein levels which point to the reason the fat and calcium are building in the coronary arteries.

People are not just concerned regarding heart disease, and rightly so. For non–smoking males, bowel and prostate cancers are also major concerns. There is no general agreement as to the role of screening for these conditions.

Again, the less expensive method of screening for bowel cancer is a rectal examination and a test for occult blood in the bowel motions. This method although inexpensive does miss cancers and again it is my opinion that adults over 40 should have at least one colonoscopy in their lifetime. This test is essential for people with a family history of bowel cancer and in this case should be performed every three to five years.

Calcium in the arteries acts as a scaffold to protect the artery walls from rupture.

Screening women for breast and cervical cancer is vital. Most authorities agree that mammography should be performed routinely in women over 50 but there is still conjecture in the 40 to 50 age group. Pap smear testing for cervical cancer is a must and should be performed at least every two years.

Bone densitometry is a useful, non–invasive method for assessing the degree of osteoporosis. Fractures, especially involving the spine and hips can be debilitating for many women as they age. The earlier preventative programs can be instituted the better.

Diabetes is a common disorder and a major risk for all forms of vascular disease. The early detection and management of diabetes is vital to prevent the disastrous complications. If you are at risk for diabetes it would be advisable to have your doctor conduct a screening test.

I believe advanced screening methods, to be introduced over the next ten years, will make it possible to accurately detect common cancers at their earliest stages. Knowledge of the disease is vital and early detection can act as a strong stimulus to commence and follow through with disease fighting and health promoting programs.

As the Human Genome Project (mapping of the entire DNA sequence) draws towards its completion we can see that in the future, health assessments will involve genetic screening. This will allow us to detect at an early stage an individual's lifelong risk for common diseases. Strategies will then be introduced at an early stage, to arrest or reverse their progress. The next 20 years should really see an amazing revolution in preventative medicine.

One excellent method to assess your current risk for heart disease is High Speed Coronary Gated Computerised Tomography (HSCGCT), scanning of the coronary arteries. This rapid, simple, completely non–invasive scan takes accurate images of the coronary arteries looking for coronary calcium. Calcium accumulates in the arteries as a response to fat build–up and there is a direct link between the amount of calcium and the amount of fat. It is my opinion that the most effective screening method for coronary artery disease (our biggest killer) is HSCGCT.

There are now a number of studies showing that the calcium score (a computer generated number to indicate the area and density of calcium in your arteries) is an accurate predictor of future risk for a vascular event.

A score of 0 implies a very low risk

A score of 1 to 100 implies a low risk

A score of 100 to 400 is a moderate risk

A score above 400 is a higher risk.

For example, one study showed a score greater than 160 predicted a risk for a vascular event such as a heart attack as being 10 times higher than that predicted by high cholesterol.

Donald Martin is 50 years old. He is an excellent tennis player and a hard working lawyer. His father, however, died of a heart attack at 45. Donald had heard from a friend that CT scanning of the heart is an excellent screening test for heart disease and despite the fact that he felt perfectly well, he attended my Sydney clinic to have his scan.

He was shocked to find his score was 1220. He immediately underwent stress echocardiography (an ultrasound of the heart before and after exercise) and the front wall of his heart stopped after exercise, despite the fact that he had no symptoms.

An angiogram was performed which showed a 100% block in his left anterior descending artery, a 90% block in his circumflex and moderate disease in the remaining arteries. He then underwent urgent coronary artery bypass surgery. I put it to you that without this initial test he would have probably dropped dead on the tennis court at some stage over the next few months.

So what test should you have and at what age? Study the Health Test Chart to see what you should be doing.

Category	Tests	Disease Process Screened
<40 y.o	coronary artery calcium	coronary artery disease
	scoring (cacs)	if strong family history
	(high speed ct scanning)	
	mammography	breast cancer
		if strong family history
	regular pap smears	cervical cancer
	blood pressure	general check-up
	cholesterol profile	
	HIV, hepatitis screen	
Male > 40 y.o.	coronary artery	coronary artery disease
	calcium score	
	full cardiac pathology	
	psa	prostate cancer
	hiv, hepatitis screen	AIDS, hepatitis
	colonoscopy	bowel cancer
Female 40-50	mammography	breast cancer
Females > 50 y.o.	mammography	
	Pap smears	
	bone densitometry	osteoporosis
	cacs	
	full cardiac pathology	
	colonoscopy	bowel cancer

CHAPTER FIVE

ANTIOXIDANTS THE STORY

Let us now look at the science of antioxidants, noting that I will present evidence regarding individual vitamins in the chapters covering these vitamins. This explanation of antioxidants is going to get a little technical, stick with me. It is in your interest to understand the free radical and antioxidant story.

Free radicals

Firstly, we must ask what free radicals are and, if they are so bad for us, why did nature allow them in the first place? Free radicals are unstable chemicals that are generated when the body is exposed to stress. This stress can be anything from pollution, saturated fat to any of the numerous chemicals that are daily pumped through our bodies or even due to excessive exercise or physical injuries. The chemicals released during these situations react with our universal energy supply of oxygen. This forms oxygen based free radicals.

Free radicals are unstable electrons damaging cells, protein, DNA and collagen within our bodies.

Free radicals are compounds that are short one electron and therefore are unstable. They travel around the body looking for stable chemicals from which they steal electrons and thus become stable. Isn't it interesting how everything in nature craves stability, including us!

Once that electron is stolen, the initial stable body chemical becomes unstable or oxidised. Unfortunately, the most common targets for these nasty little critters (free radicals) are the linings of blood vessels, LDL cholesterol (bad cholesterol) and DNA. It is this oxidisation process that sets us up for heart disease and cancer, the two biggest killers in Western society.

The first change that occurs in heart disease (long before we develop blockages in our coronary arteries) is damage and loss of function to the endothelium (the lining of the blood vessel walls). When our body is subjected to any danger (the so–called fear, fight, flight system), we need maximum blood flow to our muscles so we can either defend ourselves or, for the more sensible coward's, run! The way this is achieved by the body is with a substance known as nitric oxide (NO). Nitric oxide is made in the endothelium (blood vessel lining) and is the major dilating (blood vessel opening) substance in the body.

When we are in a deep sleep at night the last thing we need is torrential blood flow to our muscles wasting all that energy. Therefore nature has created the opposite blood vessel constricting chemical known as endothelin, thus reducing the blood flow to our muscles and conserving energy. In both scenarios of danger and rejuvenation, the body is geared for survival, through either protection from danger or conservation of energy.

If our bodies become overloaded with free radicals, our natural antioxidant system may not be strong enough to cope. When this is the case, free radicals are left to go on causing their own form of destruction. They damage the lining of the blood vessels by ripping out their stable electrons. In the same way, they also damage the LDL cholesterol, causing it to become deposited in the walls of our blood vessels (without this free radical attack, LDL cholesterol is basically harmless). Free radicals also oxidise the DNA making it send abnormal chemical instruction to the cells, therefore increasing the risk of cancer.

Our only defence to this free radical oxidisation of our vital chemicals and cells is through antioxidants. Antioxidants act as decoys to free radicals, sacrificing their own electrons to protect our body's vital structures. The body has its own inherent antioxidant system, which generally copes with the day–to–day free radical attacks. These internal or endogenous antioxidants are usually manufactured within the body. However, there is also an essential supply of antioxidants that we receive from foods. These work in concert with the body's

Tobacco, pollutants and agricultural sprays produce free radicals in the body.

production. Antioxidants derived from nature are not manufactured to any extent in the body. I believe we owe it to ourselves to overcome free radical attack with the use of foods high in antioxidants and antioxidant supplementation.

As humans evolved, survival was absolutely dependent on living in harmony and perfect balance with nature. Unfortunately, since the Industrial Revolution and especially over the second half of the twentieth century, the explosion of science and technology has outstripped our body's ability to cope in a polluted world.

I have many patients who complain about taking prescribed drugs. When I ask their reasons for not wanting to take these medications, they say, 'I don't like putting unnatural chemicals into my body!' My response to this is, 'Are you breathing? Did you use deodorant today? Do you use make–up?'

Almost every act of cleaning from washing clothes, dishes to cleaning our teeth uses chemicals. We are being exposed to micro and macro doses of chemicals every second of the day in some form or another and despite this, we are living longer than almost all previous generations.

One of the greatest forms of hypocrisy is the cigarette smoker who refuses to take drugs because of the possible side effects of the chemicals in the drugs. The smoking of one cigarette produces three trillion free radicals in your blood stream.

One of the huge advantages of modern society is longevity but as you know there is no free lunch. With longevity goes increasing years of free radical exposure and therefore increased susceptibility to free radical induced diseases. Living in modern society with its vast array of chemicals and poisons means ever increasing numbers of free radicals, and therefore ever increasing rates of free radical based diseases.

Let's talk anecdotes (which are definitely not science but let's face it – a good story is worth 1,000 scientific papers). How many people are you hearing of these days with premature heart disease? How often do we hear of the 45 year old, seemingly very fit person, who dropped dead during his morning jog? How many women are developing breast cancer at an early age? The figures quoted these days suggest one in 11 women will develop breast cancer at some stage in their life.

Free radicals are associated with aging. Antioxidants stage a counter attack by scavenging the free radicals.

Antioxidants

Our bodies make their own antioxidants which are effective to a point, but we need to supplement this system with external sources of antioxidants.

There are five sources of antioxidants available:
1. Extra virgin olive oil
2. Tea
3. Fruit and vegetables
4. Red wine
5. Antioxidant dose vitamins

Extra virgin olive oil

This oil is from the first pressing of the olives. This is the natural, purest olive oil. We have been deluded (through clever advertising) into believing whenever the word 'lite' (spelt incorrectly) is on the side of a bottle or food packet, that it must be better for you. In the case of olive oil, the 'lite' version basically has had all the antioxidants stripped out of it. The long–living people of Crete cook in extra virgin olive oil, add it to their salads and dip their bread in it (they don't use butter or margarine). As we have shown, the people of Crete have little heart disease, cancer or diabetes. I'm not suggesting this is all due to extra virgin olive oil but it certainly contributes to a significant proportion of the energy in the their diet.

Tea

Tea is an excellent source of antioxidants. It is loaded with bioflavonoids in the form of tannins. Around 30% of the antioxidant intake in the Australian diet comes from tea. So going over to grandma's house for a cup of tea isn't just great because it is family bonding.

Fruit and vegetables

There are 600 naturally occurring antioxidants in fruits and vegetables. The benefits of consumption of fruit and vegetables are endless. Many epidemiological studies have demonstrated an inverse relationship between the consumption of fruit and vegetables, and heart disease and cancer.

Red wine

My favourite antioxidant is that magical fluid, red wine. Although many studies of alcohol consumption have demonstrated a reasonable benefit across the board for moderate drinking (10–50% decrease in cardiovascular disease). There appears to be a much greater and consistent benefit demonstrated in the studies that focused on red wine. Two large studies were done, the first was known as the Copenhagen Heart Study. It followed 13,000 Danes for 12 years examining four separate groups of teetotallers, beer drinkers, spirit drinkers and wine drinkers. We are talking here of an average consumption of two to three standard drinks per day.

1 standard drink of beer =   285 mls
1 standard nip of spirits =   30 mls
1 standard drink of wine =   100 mls

The beer drinkers had no benefit or detriment over the teetotallers. The spirit drinkers, surprisingly, had 30% more heart disease and cancer. The wine drinkers had 50% less heart disease and cancer.

The second large study, specifically examining red wine consumption comes from Serge Renaud's group in France. I bet you couldn't guess that from his name! This study showed that the best dose of red wine for this amazing 50% reduction in heart disease and cancer was 200 mls or two standard drinks per day.

> *There are 600 naturally occurring antioxidants in fruits and vegetables.*

Although the heart disease rate stayed low with increasing levels of wine consumption, the cancer and cirrhosis rate rose through the roof with over four standard drinks per day. The reality is, alcohol consumption above four standard drinks per day is a poison to the body and cannot be recommended under any circumstances. I have five very strong recommendations:

1. 200 mls of red wine per day is the correct dose
2. You do not get double the benefit from double the dose
3. You cannot save up all your alcohol for Friday or Saturday nights. Drink a little daily
4. Red wine is best when sipped slowly with a lovely Mediterranean style meal, enjoyed with your loved ones
5. At least one in 20 people in any community are alcoholics and should not consume any alcohol

Red wine contains the three strongest antioxidants known to man and 250 mls per day can switch off 95% of the free radical attack on your LDL cholesterol.

Antioxidant dose vitamins.

In our 'modern' world there is an increased output of polluting chemicals, altering of our food for flavour and longer life as well as for pest and disease resistance. We are also exposed to previously unknown bacteria and viruses.

The 'new' sources of attack are:
1. Pollution
2. Additives, preservatives and food colourings
3. Pesticides, herbicides and insecticides
4. Genetically modified foods and antibiotics in meat
5. Bacteria, viruses and parasites.

Pollution

Those of us who live in or near large cities (which is now the majority of us) are breathing in polluted air. I was once lecturing in Manchuria, China, in a city that is one of the most industrialised cities in the world. I had finished lecturing in a hospital and was standing outside chatting with one of the Chinese cardiologists. I was holding a white piece of paper, and after a ten minute chat, I looked down to see this paper was almost black from pollution. You could wipe black soot off your forehead and I felt short of breath just walking along the streets.

The amount of free radicals in our bodies from pollution is enormous. We certainly do not derive enough antioxidants from our diet to overcome these poisonous chemicals.

Additives, preservatives and food colourings

Although I cannot quantify the free radicals generated by the additives, preservatives, food colourings and other assorted micro–doses of poisons that end up on our dinner plates, I know they can wreak havoc with susceptible individuals.

Pesticides, herbicides and insecticides

These days even our wonderful fruit and vegetables have different chemicals, often in the form of pest and disease sprays to improve crop yield. I have always wondered about the term 'safe level of poison'. What is a safe level of poison – this sounds like an extraordinary oxymoron if ever I heard one!

GMF and antibiotics in meat

Despite repeated denials from the industries involved, do we really know what is being fed to our animals in terms of antibiotics, muscle building supplements, and heaven forbid, genetically modified material? I am not accusing any one particular group of a conspiracy, but have wondered why the last generation of children appear (on the whole) taller than their parents. It certainly can't be the genes, as genetic evolution takes much longer than one to two generations!

Bacteria, viruses and parasites

Since the arrival of HIV–AIDS and the many other super bugs, medical science has realised that new viruses are evolving that are resistant to our usual treatments. Bacterium are developing resistance to antibiotics. Our immune systems are constantly being challenged by a rapidly changing world.

It is for all these reasons, coupled with the burgeoning scientific data that we will explore in the next chapter, that the case for antioxidant dose vitamins is compelling. I believe with the increasing longevity of our population and the reasonable demand for a better quality of life, the consumption of antioxidants in food, wine and as supplements is a vital component of optimum health.

CHAPTER SIX

THE EVIDENCE FOR ANTIOXIDANTS

Is there any real science behind antioxidant dose vitamins preventing disease and possibly prolonging life? Well, the short answer is yes. There is scientific evidence that strongly suggests they will work for you but, as with most aspects of human existence, there is no definite proof.

I can understand why the general public is becoming increasingly cynical regarding much of the 'scientific advice' we are being given.

If you eat a lot of margarine consider taking vitamin E to reduce the oxidation of this reactive fat.

Take, for example, the area of nutrition. How many times have we heard from the nutrition police that a certain food is good for you, only to find later it would poison a rock wallaby, or vice versa. Take, for example, margarine. When margarine was introduced in the 1920s as a replacement for butter, the rates of cardiovascular disease began to plummet. These amazing polyunsaturated fats helped drop the bad cholesterol levels, which they continue to do to this day.

With the drop in heart disease we have seen a rise in asthma and arthritis, two very common chronic inflammatory disorders. Some researchers believe this is due to the widespread use of omega–6 polyunsaturated fats, the common fats used in many margarines and vegetable oils. You can't win, can you! Interestingly, new margarines are being made with the good fats, the monounsaturated and the omega–3 polyunsaturated fats. These are anti–inflammatory, unlike the omega–6 polyunsaturated fats.

Nutrition experts have told us for many years that we should avoid nuts. There are now five major studies that all suggest the ingestion of five nut–based meals (15 to 20 nuts per meal) per week reduces your risk for cardiac disease by a whopping 50%. Hang on, you say, nuts are full of fat and fats are bad for me. The reality of this health message is that not all fats are bad and it's in fact better to eat a good fat diet rather than a low fat diet. However, there are still many people in the world of preventative health who cling to this unproven notion that low fat diets are the cornerstone of eating well.

There is no doubt that a diet high is saturated fat is detrimental and a low fat diet is better. In terms of cardiac and cancer prevention, the evidence is strongly in favour of a diet high in monounsaturated and omega–3 polyunsaturated fats.

If we look at the current levels of scientific knowledge we can, I believe, make some reasonable assumptions. It will not be difficult for you to decide that the consumption of antioxidant dose vitamins is useful. They are an important adjunct to a healthy lifestyle.

Antioxidant Research

I have attended far too many drug launches. I have heard of the wonderful benefits and low side effect profile of the latest wonder medication, only to find when I prescribed it (with caution) that it does have side effects and should be monitored very carefully. Drugs have metabolic effects and can have powerful side effects. In research, drugs usually show a significant effect in short term trials.

Antioxidant dose vitamins are generally much less powerful agents than your usual medications. They are not a quick fix, and fortunately have minimal side effects. Therefore they should not necessarily be studied with the same approach as the stronger, quicker acting pharmaceutical agents. With any medication, vitamin, surgical technique or other intervention there are five methods of assessment:

1. Laboratory evidence
2. Animal experimentation
3. Epidemiologic studies
4. Clinical trials – usually blinded and randomised
5. Clinical experience.

Laboratory Evidence

There is solid scientific evidence regarding the action of antioxidant dose vitamins in the test tube. Free radicals attack different stable body components, stealing their electrons and immediately making them unstable. Common sites of attack are:

◆ DNA (thereby increasing your risk for cancer)
◆ White cells (thereby reducing the immune system's effectiveness)
◆ Endothelial cells (damaging the cell lining the blood vessels)
◆ LDL cholesterol (the bad cholesterol) allowing the passage of oxidised fat into the blood vessel wall creating the fatty (or atherosclerotic) plaque, which is the primary lesion in the generation of almost all forms of vascular disease.

Free radicals, by stealing electrons, oxidise these different body components. If you leave your car down at the beach for a few months the salt water will rust the car – this process is known as oxidisation. This oxidisation process in our bodies is prevented by antioxidants.

Allow me to use the example of the blood vessel and the big three antioxidants – vitamin E, vitamin C and beta–carotene.

Vitamin E (a fat soluble vitamin) forms a protective shield around LDL cholesterol, preventing free radical attack on the LDL. Vitamin E sacrifices itself by donating one of its electrons. The vitamin E then temporarily becomes a pro–oxidant (or a free radical itself). That is until vitamin C (a water soluble molecule that travels around in the fluid component of the blood known as the plasma), in turn donates one of its electrons to vitamin E, thus returning vitamin E to its original antioxidant state.

As a further safeguard, the third major antioxidant, beta–carotene sits in the wall of the blood vessel preventing the uptake of oxidised LDL, thereby preventing the formation of fatty plaque.

The protective effects of vitamin E, vitamin C and beta–carotene in cultured cells in the laboratory are well accepted scientific facts. The body manufactures its own antioxidants and these, combined with vitamins E, C and beta–carotene work in synergy to prevent free radical attack.

Animal experimentation

Around 23 separate studies have been performed on animals using various forms of antioxidant dose vitamins. Eighteen have been positive, showing a significant benefit from antioxidants (particularly in preventing vascular disease). The other five studies have shown no benefit.

Vitamins C and E are essential for the cell walls of the arteries to resist the attachment of LDL cholesterol.

What basically happened in these studies was either rabbits, hamsters, mice and, in two studies, monkeys were given a high saturated fat diet to induce rapid atherosclerosis (fat build up in the lining of the arteries). Half the animals were given an antioxidant dose vitamin and the other half acted as the control group. Their arteries were then examined.

In the vast majority of studies, the antioxidants used, markedly reduced the development of atherosclerosis. The interesting point regarding animal experimentation is that a high (bad) fat diet in experimental animals can induce atherosclerosis in a few months. The equivalent diet in humans can take between 20 to 40 years to induce the same disease that takes only a few months in an animal.

A recent study performed on rats shows enormous promise for the future of vitamin E. Vitamin E in the diet is mainly in the gamma form. In supplement form it is usually in the alpha form. This study showed that both forms given to two groups of rats compared with control rats significantly:

1. Thinned the blood by stopping the platelets (the sticky cells in the blood which form clots) from clumping together
2. Reduced the amount of blockages within the arteries

3. Markedly reduced the free radical attack
4. Markedly increased the body's own endogenous antioxidants
5. Reduced the tendency for atherosclerosis formation

Unfortunately, the researchers used doses in the rats that would be toxic to humans, so similar studies need to be performed using more acceptable doses with either type of vitamin E, looking more at the clinical endpoints.

I have used the same argument for the human trials of antioxidant dose vitamins. Although they work rapidly in animals, it may take 15 to 20 years to see results on humans.

One of the very exciting innovations developed recently in Europe is the artificial gut. This amazing piece of technology allows drugs to be tested in this simulated environment, thus preventing the need for animal experimentation.

Epidemiologic studies

Epidemiology is the study of populations. No attempt is made to control the population (there are obviously no bureaucrats involved). A population is then observed for their various characteristics over a long period of time.

One of the most famous epidemiologic studies is the Seven Countries Study, which was conducted over a 10 year period. Countries as varied as Japan, Finland and the island of Crete were studied for their dietary habits, lifestyle factors and rates of disease. Some astounding facts emerged. The Japanese diet consisting of around 25% fat with only 7% saturated fat, produced some very low rates of heart disease. This study provided one of the first links between saturated fat intake and heart disease. The areas studied in Finland and Scotland had the highest rates of heart disease corresponding with their (at that time) dietary intake of fat, which approached 50% of their energy intake. The majority of this fat was saturated fat.

The most surprising fact that emerged from this study was the very low rates of heart disease in Crete, in fact, the lowest in the study, even lower than Japan. This was despite the fact that the average fat intake in the Cretan diet was 40%, (most of that fat was from the good fat – monounsaturated fat) usually in the form of extra virgin olive oil. Despite the fact that this evidence was available in the 1970s, it has only been recently that the medical world has begun to embrace the benefits of the consumption of good fats.

The major criticism of epidemiologic studies is the lack of control of all the variables. For example, Crete is mainly an agricultural island with little technology, especially during the

study period, and the inhabitants of Crete consumed a very distinct diet and were more active than the other populations studied. The detractors of these studies argue that it may be the exercise and not the diet. Maybe it is the entire lifestyle such as the afternoon siesta or the close–knit community living that makes the difference.

The two most famous epidemiologic studies reviewing vitamin intake have been the Nurses' Health Study and the Male Health Professionals' Study. Many lifestyle, supplement and assorted therapies have been studied in both these groups over a prolonged period of time.

The Nurse's study followed around 87,000 nurses over an eight year period, and found a 41% reduction in cardiac events in those nurses taking between 100–500 IU of alpha–tocopherol (vitamin E) per day. Interestingly in the Iowa Women's Study of 36,000 women over 12 years, there was no obvious benefit from supplementation, but a significant reduction in cardiac events in those women consuming a diet high in vitamin E.

The Male Health Professionals' Study over a similar period showed a 36% reduction in cardiac events with vitamin E supplementation, but no benefit or detriment with beta–carotene. Another study from the United States, known as NHANES, reviewed around 11,000 men and women and showed an inverse relationship between mortality from heart disease and vitamin C intake.

Laboratory work, animal experimentation and epidemiologic studies all suggest the benefits of antioxidant dose vitamins as an adjunct to good health.

Clinical trials

The medical profession demands the results of clinical trials. These trials range from small studies, identifying biochemical or blood vessel effects, to large trials involving many people over a long period of time.

In 1997 researchers from Ann Arbor (Michigan), University of California (San Diego) and the University of Rochester (NY State) demonstrated that a cocktail of antioxidant dose vitamins gave you expensive blood and not just expensive urine. They tried various combinations of vitamin E, vitamin C and beta–carotene. They measured antioxidant ability by a test known as 'lag phase' and found, over 12 weeks, the high dose group demonstrated a significant antioxidant response. The mid–dose group was not strong enough to demonstrate a response.

The mid–dose and high dose groups were as follows:

	Mid dose	High dose
vitamin E	400 IU	800 IU
vitamin C	500 mgs	1,000 mgs
beta–carotene	12 mgs	25 mgs

MEASUREMENT   OF   LIPID   PEROXIDATION

DISEASES LINKED TO FREE RADICAL DAMAGE

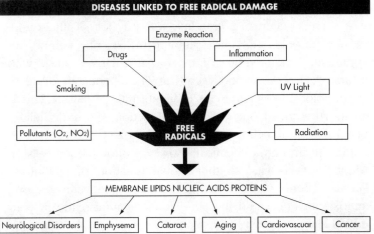

This is an important study in many respects:

◆ It is demonstrating the importance of the dose with anti–oxidant dose vitamins. Some people blindly swallow a 'multivitamin', or some supplement that has been marketed with a clever name, without realising that there has not been great attention to quality control or dosing and then expect to derive some benefit. This study is a strong guide to the dose of vitamins we should be taking.

◆ It highlights the concept of the antioxidant package. Most studies test either one or two vitamins without regard to the entire antioxidant system. As I have stated, most controlled trials to date have failed to demonstrate a clear benefit from the use of antioxidant dose vitamins, because they usually involve vitamin E and beta–carotene (in the wrong dosing schedule) or vitamin E alone.

◆ This study also demonstrates a sustained benefit from the ongoing consumption of antioxidant dose vitamins, rather than giving a subject just one dose of three antioxidants. Even though the study was maintained for only 12 weeks, it still demonstrated a benefit.

Another study from the *Journal of the American College of Cardiology* approached the assessment of antioxidant dose vitamins from another angle. You will remember your mother or grandmother telling you when you were a child that you shouldn't swim within a half hour of eating. You thought she was a nag, but in fact grandma was physiologically sound, despite probably not understanding the science behind her argument. When we eat a meal (particularly a meal with saturated fat), our blood vessels ability to open or dilate to supply blood to our muscles is significantly impaired. This is an impairment of our endothelial function, the endothelium being the single cell layer that lines our blood vessels. This is mediated through a chemical known as nitric oxide (or NO). Nitric oxide is vital to the normal function of our blood vessels. There is a very strong interaction between a strong antioxidant effect and the generation of nitric oxide in your endothelium.

If you eat a fatty meal, you don't make as much nitric oxide and you will not deliver enough blood to your muscles to allow appropriate exercise. Therefore grandma's comments were correct. American researchers using this, took an experimental and control group and fed them both a fatty meal (you guessed it from a popular take–away food outlet) and demonstrated a 50% reduction in endothelial function, or in other words, there was 50% less nitric oxide released. One group received placebo treatment and the other group received vitamin E 800 IU, vitamin C 1,000 mgs and beta–carotene 25 mgs. The group taking antioxidant dose vitamins had normal endothelial function despite the fatty meal.

I am not suggesting we should therefore rush down to our favourite take–away outlet and buy any of their fat–laden treats, surreptitiously slipping in the antioxidant cocktail beforehand and all will be well. Antioxidants are good protection, but they do not counter the bad effects of eating saturated fats.

I am reminded of the 100 kg man who walks into the take–away food store requesting a hamburger, fries and a cup of coffee, while puffing away on his cigarette. Then he takes

...AND A SIDE ORDER OF VITAMIN E, MATE. GOTTA LOOK AFTER THE OL' TICKER!

a vitamin E out of his pocket and says to the bemused person behind the counter 'I'm taking vitamin E. It's important to look after my ticker you know.'

These research studies demonstrate that antioxidant dose vitamins do work as a one–off protection, even over the short term. However, I believe they are not a substitute for good healthy lifestyle practices.

The double blind control clinical trial

What about the 'holy grail', the double blind control trial? Is there any evidence supporting the long term use of antioxidants? I must state that most of the trials to date have been disappointing in their results and also in their design.

The best example is a trial of vitamin E and beta–carotene performed in Finland. The trial went for eight years (not long enough for the study of antioxidants). Cholesterol lowering agents have very powerful effects on metabolism. Antioxidant dose vitamins are useful, though much less strong adjuncts to a healthy lifestyle. They also show benefit for people with established diseases. For a trial to show a true benefit of antioxidants, it should run for between 15 to 20 years (especially to show the benefits for people without established diseases). It's a bit like superannuation. You pay in now and get the benefits down the track.

The second aspect of the trial concerns the doses of antioxidant supplements used. This trial consisted of only 50 IU of Vitamin E and 15 mgs of beta–carotene daily. The vitamin E dose is far too small to expect any real clinical benefit. Fifty IUs is barely above any sort of recommended daily allowance and certainly not in true antioxidant doses.

Finally, and most importantly, was the population studied. This trial studied the effects of vitamin E and beta–carotene on 29,000 Finnish smokers. This trial in fact showed a slight but statistically proven increase in lung cancer in the smokers who took beta–carotene when compared to those taking a placebo.

This trial was designed for failure. It used inappropriate doses, inappropriate length of study and worse still, an inappropriate study group. Fancy suggesting that any treatment could overcome the noxious effects of cigarette smoke!

In a somewhat similar trial reviewed in the May 1996 *New England Journal of Medicine*, there was no benefit from the combination of beta–carotene 30 mgs per day and vitamin A 25,000 IU over four years in around 18,000 men aged between 45 to 69 years. The disappointment from this trial was on several levels.

◆ First was the slight increase in lung cancer and cardio–vascular disease in the people receiving the vitamin therapy.

◆ Secondly, these men were either smokers or former smokers with a history of asbestos exposure.

◆ Finally the trial was stopped after four years because of the adverse results. This trial, with the unfortunate name of the CARET Study, concluded that beta–carotene and vitamin A in supplement form might have an adverse effect on the risk for lung cancer and cardiovascular disease.

I must say I would be much more concerned about their exposure to asbestos and cigarette smoke. This trial again exposes the futility of studying antioxidant dose vitamins in an unhealthy section of the community and then trying to extrapolate the results to the rest of the population.

The dosing schedule was unusual and it is my opinion that beta–carotene and vitamin A should not be used in isolation as supplements especially as cigarette smoke (which generates three trillion free radicals with every cigarette smoked) makes beta–carotene pro–oxidant. To understand this principle is to understand the basic mode of action of antioxidants. Vitamin E and vitamin C have much greater flexibility than beta–carotene in their ability to be antioxidants. They donate an electron to a free radical, which then makes either molecule (E or C) unstable and therefore temporarily pro–oxidant, until they are returned to their antioxidant state by the body's own antioxidant mechanisms. This reaction is not as forthcoming with beta–carotene, and if it is overwhelmed by free radicals (as is the case with cigarette smoking), then it is more difficult for it to change back from the induced pro–oxidant state. Thus, the solution is not to damn beta–carotene, but rather, not to use it as a supplement in isolation, nor use it with cigarette smoking.

Beta–carotene is found in yellow fruit and vegetables.

In the Male Physicians Trial beta–carotene was used in isolation in a rather bizarre dose of 50 mgs on alternate days in 22,000 male doctors aged 40–84 years old. In this group 11% were smokers and 40% former smokers. They were followed for 12 years. During this time there was no benefit or harm shown from this isolated dosing schedule in regard to cancer, cardiovascular disease or death. At the worst, beta–carotene produced no harm and is of no use.

A study known as the Linxian Trial looked at 30,000 rural Chinese who were probably nutritionally deficient. Eight different combinations of vitamins were trialed and the most effective was the grouping of beta–carotene, vitamin E and selenium. This showed a significant reduction in cancer during the study period.

This is difficult to extrapolate to Western society as we are considering a group of people who were probably deficient in some of the nutrients used for supplementation. You can't win can you!

My opinion from analysing these trials in regard to beta–carotene is as follows:

1. Don't take beta–carotene in isolation
2. Don't smoke and take beta–carotene
3. Antioxidant dose vitamin trials need to be extended to somewhere between 15 to 20 years
4. A correct dose of beta–carotene needs to be established but, if you are thinking of long term supplement action, at this stage I would suggest between 12 to 25 mgs per day

I have argued that we cannot always rely on the results of these large studies and that aspects of the so–called 'evidence–based' approach can be flawed. Many of these studies are based around statistics and, what seems like a dramatic effect, may only be very small when you examine the true numbers. It has been said that 58% of statistics are made up on the spot. Some day an insightful statistician will figure out the time lost in compiling statistics. You, as an intelligent consumer of knowledge, need to read, listen and decide for yourself what you should be doing.

Alright Everybody...whatever you're working on... today's statistic is 58%!

Clinical Experience

The reality is that 80% of the medicine practiced by doctors is experienced–based. I am sure you would prefer a doctor to treat you based on his or her vast experience, rather than a pharmaceutical sponsored trial that has just hit the journals.

What I am sharing with you in this book comes from clinical experience in my busy cardiology practice and also from my constant study of the topic. As a cardiologist, my focus is on heart disease prevention, early detection with early intervention. I am sharing with you what my patients have found to work for them. The antioxidant story is not about a quick fix. It is about combining correct lifestyle with a consistently reinforced antioxidant counter attack on the marauding free radicals.

Since commencing high speed CT scanning of the heart, I have seen numerous patients with strong risk factors for heart disease such as high cholesterol, high blood pressure and even marked elevation in Lp(a) with strong family histories of heart disease. These people should all have had at least evidence of significant atherosclerosis, if not established heart disease. Amazingly, there are some who defy that trend and usually they are the ones who have been living a healthy lifestyle and taking multiple antioxidant therapies for many years.

Just the other day, I saw a 73 year old man with a high cholesterol, an elevated Lp(a) and a strong family history of heart disease. Basically all the odds were loaded against him. We were both surprised and delighted when his coronary calcium score was zero. He had been taking antioxidants for 30 years and, of course, leading a healthy lifestyle. His risk for a future heart attack or stroke was extremely low despite his age. This was his lucky day.

CHAPTER SEVEN

VITAMINS E AND C, BLOOD BROTHERS

Vitamin E

When I started medical school back in the 1970s, our professors informed us that the only true function of vitamin E was to prevent sterility in rats. I remember the vivid picture of this parade of infertile rats making nocturnal visits to the local health food store to raid the vitamin E supplies. I also remember a pamphlet I read in the 70s expounding the virtue of Vitamin E for all forms of vascular disease, thinking at the time how deluded this alternate looney must have been.

Although the medical profession has not come full circle, and are still trotting out the usual scientific cautionary comments like, 'Although this study of vitamin E shows promise, there is still no evidence for the widespread use in the community.' Tell that to the rat population. Can you imagine how much 1,000 IU of vitamin E would fetch on the rat black market?

In all seriousness, the evidence for the benefit of vitamin E is very strong. Sure there have been a number of studies that have been neutral in demonstrating a benefit from vitamin E, but as I have stressed in the preceding chapter, this is almost certainly due to one of the three main factors:

♦ The wrong dose
♦ The wrong study period – always too short in people without disease
♦ The wrong population studied

An important point to make here is the difference between primary and secondary prevention. Primary prevention is the prevention of a certain disease in a supposedly healthy (although possibly high risk) group of people. For example, the West of Scotland Cholesterol Study was a primary prevention trial. This trial examined a large group of asymptomatic (people without symptoms) middle aged men with high blood cholesterol levels, who had not as yet experienced a heart attack or any other heart problems. Half were given a cholesterol lowering pill and the other half a placebo. They were then followed for a period of time, mainly looking at their death rates and their heart attack rates.

This is primary prevention research and it requires larger numbers for long periods of time, as people who enter the study without disease generally have low rates of disease when followed for a period of less than ten years. If, however, you take people with established disease (secondary prevention) then they have a higher risk for repeat problems with that disease and, therefore, the event rates are higher and can be expected to occur more quickly.

If you follow this group of men in the West of Scotland trial for five years, their event rate for combined death and heart attack is less than 5% over the period. If you take a group of middle aged men with a prior history of coronary heart disease and follow them for five years, their risk for death is 2% per year and therefore 10% should be dead over a five year period.

The biggest risk for heart disease is having heart disease in the first place! Therefore, secondary prevention trials give you a much bigger 'bang for your buck' because intervening at that stage has a much greater chance of benefit in a much higher risk group.

Using powerful metabolic regulators, such as cholesterol lowering drugs, has quicker, more powerful effects than using the less powerful vitamin therapy approach. Vitamin therapy takes longer to have its effects and therefore the trials should be longer.

There are five trials of vitamin therapy in progress at present, (some primary and some secondary prevention) but all are over too short a time period to truly assess the efficiency of antioxidant dose vitamins in preventing our two major free radical based diseases, cardiovascular disease and cancer.

CHAOS trial

A relatively recent trial called CHAOS (Cambridge Heart Antioxidant Study) selected a group of 2,000 people with proven heart disease (a secondary prevention trial) and treated half with either 400 or 800 IU of vitamin E. Over an average follow–up period of only 19 months there was a 77% reduction in heart attack in those taking vitamin E. There was, however, no difference in the death rates. I believe there are two reasons for this.

Firstly, there were not enough people in the study to demonstrate the mortality benefit and secondly, the trial was too short. Regardless of this lack of mortality benefit, the reduction in heart attack was striking and also very encouraging. Despite these results, the medical profession still does not recommend all patients with heart disease take vitamin E, regardless of the fact that the doses taken in the CHAOS trial have never been shown to cause any side effects. Don't forget my comment that 50% of American cardiologists take vitamin E but only 30% suggest their patients do the same.

GISSI trial

The recent GISSI trial (prevention) from Italy, examined the effect of vitamin E after a heart attack. During this short study period of only three and a half years follow up, there was no benefit from taking vitamin E. Recent research work has confirmed doses below 400 IU per day are not sufficient to prevent LDL oxidisation by free radicals. Although in this trial a correct dose was used, the study period was too short to demonstrate a benefit.

When will these research scientists get it right? Apart from the CHAOS trial (which gave a surprising result but at least used an appropriate dose of vitamin E), none of the long term trials conducted to date have been designed to give vitamin E a chance to demonstrate a significant benefit.

HOPE trial

The most recently published trial using Vitamin E has been the HOPE (Heart Outcomes Prevention Evaluation) trial. This trial followed around 9,000 people for a five year period. This was a placebo controlled trial evaluating the effects of a blood pressure drug Ramipril taken in a high dose (10 mgs) on a daily basis, and also vitamin E in a dose of 400 IU per day. This was in a group of people at high risk for cardiovascular events.

Entry into the study involved having some form of established vascular disease such as angina, prior stroke or peripheral vascular disease and around one third were diabetics. They also had to have high cholesterol, high blood pressure or some other risk factor for heart disease. All participants were over 55 years old. There was no apparent benefit in the subjects taking vitamin E over this short study period. This has brought cries from medical journalists such as 'Vitamin E a Fizzer.'

A combination of Warfarin and vitamin E may thin the blood too much.

For all the reasons I have stated, I believe this trial proves nothing. There was no mention of lifestyle modification in the study. There was only one vitamin used and the trial only went for five years.

Is there any risk from the use of vitamin E? I would suggest two areas of slight caution. Firstly, if you have high blood pressure there is the possibility of vitamin E making this worse. The answer is simple. If you have high blood pressure, start with a lower dose (somewhere between 100 to 400 IU) and have regular blood pressure check ups. If your pressure increases then there are alternative antioxidants, which may be of benefit.

Secondly, if you are on anti–coagulants such as Warfarin, there is an increase in the tendency to bleed. Warfarin is already being used to thin the blood by working on the clotting factors, which are produced in the liver. Vitamin E can affect many parameters of clotting, including the 'sticky cells' known as platelets, so the combination of Warfarin and vitamin E may thin the blood excessively. This does not mean you should never use the combination, but you should be monitored carefully.

With our present evidence, I would like to make the following five points regarding vitamin E:

♦ It is harmless apart from the caution with high blood pressure and Warfarin

♦ If you have proven heart disease, I believe the current evidence is strong enough in favour of regular consumption of vitamin E in doses ranging between 400–800 IU daily on an indefinite basis

♦ If you are at high risk for heart disease, I would strongly suggest vitamin E

♦ If you are over 35, but with minimal risk for heart disease, you will come to no harm with the regular consumption of vitamin E. However, this should be balanced with the adage, 'The lower the risk, the lower the benefit.' There is also the consideration of cost. Personally, I'd rather take the vitamin E (which I do).

♦ If you are below 35 with no risk factors for heart disease, I can see no justification for the use of vitamin E

F U N C T I O N S   O F   A N T I O X I D A N T S

ANTIOXIDANT FUNCTIONS	
VITAMIN E	
Fat-soluble phase ⟶	Chain-breaking antioxidant, Free radical scavenger, Single oxygen quencher, Efficient at high oxygen pressure
BETA-CAROTENE	
Fat-soluble phase ⟶	Single oxygen quencher, Chain-breaking antioxidant, Free radical scavenger, Efficient at low oxygen pressure
VITAMIN C	
Water-soluble phase ⟶	Free radical scavenger, Single oxygen quencher, Regeneration of vitamin E

Vitamin C

Much has been written, much has been said, many claims made for and against the benefits of Vitamin C. So, as with Vitamin E, we must examine the claims and the evidence for and against and then make our own decisions.

Twenty years ago the recommended daily allowance of all manner of vitamins and minerals was formulated. These levels were based on a group of conditions known as deficiency diseases. So if your daily intake of vitamin X or mineral Y was below the recommended daily allowance (RDA) for that particular substance, then you were at greater risk for developing the related deficiency disease. In the eighteenth century during long sea voyages, it was impossible to store fresh fruit and vegetables and the seafarers quickly developed a deficiency of vitamin C known as scurvy.

A dispute arises when certain elements of the scientific and lay community argue that we benefit from high levels of these vitamins, usually more than we can achieve from a standard modern diet. There are two aspects to this argument:

1. With modern processing, packaging, preservation and transportation, many of our foodstuffs are lacking essential vitamins and minerals, compared to eating your foods fresh from your own garden or orchard. Some groups within the scientific community suggest that only 10% of people living in Western society are receiving the recommended daily allowance of essential vitamins and minerals. One study showed that from 1985 to 1986 the average vitamin and mineral content of common fruit and vegetables had dropped by around 30% as a result of depleted soils.

2. Heart disease and cancer are the new major killers over the last 50 years. These diseases have been known about for many centuries but it is argued that, although people in Western society may have deficiencies of some vitamins and minerals, on the whole they are not undernourished and in fact most are over nourished with the macronutrients fat, protein and carbohydrates.

Changes in the composition of fruits and veggies

Mineral and vitamin content in mg per 100g

		1985	1996	change	
broccoli	calcium	103	33	minus	68%
	folic acid	47	23	minus	51%
	magnesium	24	18	minus	25%
beans	calcium	56	34	minus	39%
	folic acid	39	34	minus	13%
	magnesium	26	22	minus	15%
	vitamin B6	140	55	minus	61%
potatoes	calcium	14	4	minus	71%
	magnesium	27	18	minus	33%
	vitamin C	20	25	plus	25%
carrots	calcium	37	31	minus	16%
	magnesium	21	9	minus	57%
spinach	magnesium	62	19	minus	69%
	B6	200	82	minus	59%
	vitamin C	51	21	minus	59%
apples	calcium	7	8	plus	14%
	magnesium	5	6	minus	-20%
	vitamin C	5	1	minus	80%
bananas	calcium	8	7	minus	13%
	folic acid	23	3	minus	87%
	magnesium	31	27	minus	13%
	vitamin B6	330	22	minus	93%
strawberries	calcium	21	18	minus	14%
	magnesium	12	13	plus	8%
	vitamin C	60	13	minus	78%

Source: Black Forest Nutritional Institut "Obertal", Published in German Newspaper "Die Welt" 24/8/98

Heart disease and cancer are intimately connected to free radical exposure. Therefore the argument is that vitamins, and to a lesser extent minerals should be taken, not in doses to achieve the recommended allowances (RDAs), but in antioxidant doses to neutralise the free radicals.

It is my opinion that almost all of the clinical trials to date have either been flawed in their design or the researchers have specifically designed the trial to ensure the failure of antioxidants' ability to positively affect long term disease patterns.

Until there is a trial performed on a combination of antioxidant dose vitamins, with adequate numbers of people, over a very long period of time, using the correct doses, we are left in doubt. You either decide to wait until absolute scientific proof is available, hoping that a healthy diet will protect your body against the current free radical attack, or take the appropriate suggested doses based on the indirect scientific evidence. You don't need a prescription for antioxidant dose vitamins, it's your choice. This is one of the big objections of the medical profession, you get to choose.

Probably one of the most contentious vitamins is vitamin C, for the very reason that the results from almost all long term trials performed by mainstream medicine have not shown any clear cut results. The greatest proponent of Vitamin C was Professor Linus Pauling. Pauling was considered by mainstream medicine as somewhat of a fringe lunatic. He made rather grandiose claims for vitamin C, ranging from a cure for the common cold to a major factor in preventing heart disease and cancer. It is hard to totally dismiss the claims of a man who has won two Nobel prizes, one for science and the other for peace.

Professor Pauling was a man who practiced what he preached. It was stated, by those close to him, that he took somewhere between 10 to 30 grams of vitamin C per day. He died in his mid nineties still working 10 to 12 hours a day, up to the day of his death.

This dedicated man, felt that this most widely used vitamin played an integral part in the prevention of both heart disease and cancer. His theory as to how Vitamin C can prevent or lessen heart disease, although unproven, is a brilliant hypothesis.

The Pauling–Rath hypothesis.

Vitamin C is an essential chemical necessary for the normal function of the body. One of the most important functions of vitamin C is in the synthesis of collagen, the important protein for the connective or supportive structures of the body. Collagen is the 'cement' that gives the body its background structure holding most tissues together. Without vitamin C the body soon develops scurvy due to poorly functioning collagen. The blood vessels, become weakened and suffer bleeding into the tissues.

The Pauling–Rath hypothesis argues that when our hunter–gatherer ancestors were exposed to these repeated bouts of starvation they would experience acute vitamin C deficiency, potentially leading to weakened blood vessels. They argue that the body evolved a chemical known as Lipoprotein (a) called Lp(a). This is a large molecule with a LDL protein attached to a very large apo–protein given the name Apo(a).

The LDL cholesterol is deposited in the artery wall to stabilise the membrane. The Apo(a) causes the blood around the deposition to be slightly thicker. This then acts as a plug for any holes punched in the blood vessels by the collagen weakness. Lp(a) was therefore a survival advantage as it afforded partial protection to the lack of Vitamin C.

Another interesting aspect to the Pauling–Rath hypothesis is the associated use of L–lysine which is an amino acid. Lp(a) attaches to the blood vessel wall via the lysyl residues on the Apo(a) portion of the molecule. They say that L–lysine blocks the lysyl residue from attaching and therefore prevents the deposition of cholesterol into the artery wall.

The rural Chinese have life long cholesterol levels between 2 to 3 mmol/L and they don't develop the fat build up in their arteries (atherosclerosis). This low cholesterol level is due to the fact that around 80% of their diet is in rice and they are generally somewhat malnourished.

Atherosclerosis has the potential to develop once the total cholesterol level rises above 3 mmol/L. Mind you, your cholesterol can be 4 mmol/L and you may have severe coronary artery disease, alternatively your cholesterol could be above 7 mmol/L and you may have minimal or no disease.

Now, assuming the Pauling–Rath hypothesis is correct, with the knowledge regarding the absence of atherosclerosis below a cholesterol of 3 mmol/L, the evolution of Lipoprotein(a), shown as Lp(a), offered a survival advantage to hunter–gatherers as food was basically a survival tool rather than one of life's pleasures, as it is today. The hunter–gatherers, like the rural Chinese, had low cholesterol levels because of their diet and their lack of mechanical or assisted transport mechanisms. They had to walk or run everywhere.

Lp(a) has stayed with human beings and now levels above 0.2 mmols/L are considered abnormal, which happens to be the case for one in five people in Western society. Interestingly Lp(a) doesn't seem to be as much of a problem for black or Asian races.

As Lp(a) carries excessive bad (LDL) cholesterol and also thickens the blood, it becomes a survival disadvantage for those living in Western society. In the West the only hunter–gathering we do is jump in our cars and drive to the local supermarket. This new age hunter–gatherer takes home (by the car again) all manner of processed, packaged, chemically altered and genetically modified high fat, low fat or any fat you like, foods.

Our average cholesterol levels have risen well above the designated 3 mmol/L playing right into the hands of delighted cardiologists, ensuring people like me will be in work for years. Most of you have probably never heard of Lp(a) despite one in five of you having the stuff coursing excessively through your arteries and veins. Lp(a) is trying its best to help pay off your cardiologist's mortgage.

So what is the answer? Pauling and Rath firmly believe Lp(a) is a major factor in the epidemic of modern day coronary artery disease. Medical science is now starting to agree with them. Most of the research studies confirming around 30% of people with premature coronary artery disease having elevated levels of Lp(a).

The agreement stops there. If you ask most researchers in the field, they will tell you that there is not much you can do about Lp(a). If you were unlucky genetically with your parents, then you are stuck with the stuff in your bloodstream, so live the right lifestyle and get your cholesterol as low as possible.

Pauling and Rath, however, take a different view. Pauling saw vitamin C as an antidote to Lp(a). To take the devil's advocate position, what would you expect from a man who made it his life's work to popularise the suggestion that vitamin C was the cure for most of the world's ills? Pauling suggests mega doses of vitamin C in people with established coronary artery disease.

About 30% of people with premature coronary artery disease have elevated levels of Lp(a).

For a condition that really has minimal available medical therapy, such as a high Lp(a), I believe we should take the middle road. Instead of suggesting doses between 2 to 6 gms per day of vitamin C (as per Pauling–Rath), if I have patients with elevated levels, I suggest 2 gms per day.

The old style cholesterol lowering drug, itself a vitamin, nicotinic acid (niacin or vitamin B_3), when given in mega doses, can reduce Lp(a) usually by around 30%. Although nicotinic acid rarely reduces Lp(a) back to normal it is still useful. For women, Lp(a) often rises after menopause and therefore hormone replacement therapy (HRT) can help stabilise levels.

So what is my approach to an elevated Lp(a)? Lifestyle issues and aggressive cholesterol lowering is vitally important for people with raised Lp(a), especially if they are at high risk for or already have established coronary disease.

1. Establish knowledge of your level is the first important step. Lp(a) is not routinely measured by most doctors but – you are the consumer. You have a one in five chance of having an elevated level in your blood. Ask for the test to be done
2. If the level is above 200 mgs (0.2 mmols/L), then commence vitamin C (2 gms per day in divided doses) and L–lysine 500 mgs per day
3. Use nicotinic acid (niacin, vitamin B_3) aiming for a dose of at least 1 gm/day. Remember nicotinic acid is a prescription drug with significant side effects. There is a new controlled release preparation which is without the liver toxicity of the older slow release formulations
4. Low dose aspirin to thin the blood
5. Lifestyle measures and cholesterol lowering treatment aiming for a total cholesterol less than 4 mmol/L and an LDL cholesterol of less than 2 mmol/L

So what are the benefits from vitamin C?

1. **Collagen formation**
   Collagen is the most important substance in the connective tissue, which is the basic tissue that holds our cells together. Collagen provides the supporting network to all the body's organs and cells.
2. **Immune system**
   Vitamin C is involved in most aspects of the defence system and when the body is under stress, these requirements increase.
3. **Antioxidant system**
   Vitamin C is a water–soluble vitamin providing a vital part of the antioxidant plasma protection package.
4. **Nervous system**
   Vitamin C is vital to the normal messaging system in the brain. These messages, known as neurotransmitters, are vital for different aspects of brain function.

5. Other functions

Vitamin C is important in the production of hormones, iron absorption and many other cellular processes.

The real questions are do we get enough vitamin C in our diet and do we need more than 60 mgs per day for optimum health? A recent study from Arizona assessed the vitamin C levels of around 500 healthy, well–nourished people. Around one third were shown to have inadequate levels of vitamin C.

There have been numerous studies of the dietary consumption of Vitamin C, almost all showing a significant reduction in heart disease rates in those with the highest Vitamin C intakes. Unfortunately, to date, there have only been a handful of vitamin C supplementation studies. These studies have not been double blind, control studies but still show promising results.

The work in the cancer field is also promising. Many studies show benefits from the consumption of vitamin C and beta–carotene containing foods. The work on vitamin C supplementation is also promising. This benefit has been across the spectrum of the common cancers including lung, breast, stomach, colon and prostate. The protective effect of vitamin C seems strongest for the upper gastrointestinal cancers such as the mouth, oesophagus and larynx.

High dietary vitamin E and C supplementation also appear beneficial for many other disorders such as asthma, diabetes, cataracts and as a general tonic for the immune system.

The evidence to date is strong enough to recommend vitamin C as a daily supplement in healthy people over 35, in those at high risk for the common free radical based diseases and in those with established diseases.

Is there a downside to vitamin C supplementation? If you have a history of kidney stones (especially the common stones containing calcium oxalate) then I would suggest caution in the use of high dose vitamin C. As always, consult your doctor if you have any concerns.

Who should take vitamin C?

1. If you are less than 35 years old, without any major illnesses or in a very high risk category, there is no real justification for supplementation. Your risk is so low that the expense does not justify the benefit.

2. If you are over 35 years old, but are very healthy with no real risk factors for heart disease and cancer, you are still at low risk and should see vitamin C supplementation as an added benefit with little detriment. But again remember, the lower the risk, the lower the benefit.

3. If you are in a high risk category, such as a high cholesterol, strong family history of heart disease or cancer, then I believe vitamin C supplementation is of benefit.

4. If you have an established major diseases, the available evidence, indicates that supplementation is of benefit. Any major disease leads to increase in stress on the body and therefore an increased need for vitamins in antioxidant doses.

5. Recommended doses.
   ◆ Healthy low risk (no kidney problems) – vitamin C 500 to 1,000 mgs per day
   ◆ Heart disease, cancer – vitamin C 1 to 2 gms per day
   ◆ Special circumstances. Such as raised Lp(a) levels – vitamin C 2 gms per day

EXAMPLES VITAMIN C IN FOOD

Food	Amount	Vitamin C (mg)
Blackcurrants	1 cup	202
Red pepper, raw	1 cup, sliced	174
Guavas	1 fruit	165
Orange juice, commercial	1 cup	124
Grapefruit juice	1 cup	94
Lemons	1 fruit	83
Strawberries	1 cup	82
Green pepper	1 cup, sliced	82
Kiwi fruit, peeled	1 medium	74
Oranges	1 fruit	68
Cantaloupe melon	1 cup, diced	66
Broccoli, boiled	1/2 cup	58
Mangoes	1 fruit	57
Brussels sprouts, boiled	1/2 cup	48
Grapefruit	1/2 fruit	47
Honeydew melon	1 cup, diced	42
Raspberries	1 cup	37
Cauliflower, boiled	1/2 cup	27
Pineapples, raw	1 cup, diced	24

CHAPTER EIGHT

TO 'B' OR NOT TO 'B'

When most people talk about taking a daily vitamin preparation or some sort of 'pick–me–up tonic', they are describing a preparation which is substantially made up of the B group vitamins with some concentration of folic acid and in some cases minerals, herbs and trace elements. Is there any evidence that multivitamins (especially B and folic acid) offer advantages in addition to a healthy diet?

Initially let's look at what the functions of these vitamins are within our bodies. Vitamin B is a set of eight water soluble vitamins. There are three other substances which are not considered vitamins but are part of the B complex – choline, inositol and PABA. Water soluble vitamins are not stored in the body but are excreted in the urine. Therefore they must be taken as a daily dose in the right combination.

Vitamin B is essential for many cellular mechanisms and severe deficiencies can lead to serious diseases such as beri–beri, pellagra or different types of anaemia. It is interesting that excess doses of one B group vitamin can deplete levels of the other B vitamins. Illness and stress can also deplete B group vitamins. Vitamin B is found in a variety of foods

- ◆ Nuts, legumes
- ◆ Avocado
- ◆ Whole grains
- ◆ Organ meats
- ◆ Leafy green vegetables

Stress

Nature's clever design invented the stress response as a survival mechanism. In those prehistoric days before television, computers and mobile phones (how did one survive?), life's stresses were different. Attack from neighbouring tribes, sabre tooth tigers or visits from

Neanderthal tax collectors prompted the ancient Homo sapien to evolve the 'fear–fight–flight' system.

Basically, when confronted by any danger, the ancient harbinger of our current peaceful, harmonious society had two choices – stay and defend or run. Both choices require the same physiologic response in the body. This can be summarised as heightened brain awareness and increased blood flow to the muscles, leading to an alert person ready for either action or a fast exit.

This acute increase in brain and muscle function, although assisting in the main survival function of the human being, does come at a price. The price is an acute increase in nutrient utilisation. This is no problem if it is occasional. A high level of stress is one of the big problems in our modern society. Over the last 50 years, burgeoning technology, business demands and an increasingly competitive society mean that our stresses are not just one off acute events.

Let's do lunch!

The stress of modern society is chronic, in your face and often in your back. It is argued by many that this type of stress is a major factor in the generation of our common lethal diseases, such as heart disease and cancer. This chronic stress not only generates free radicals but also markedly depletes the B group vitamins. Conservative health professionals argue that we obtain all the micronutrients we need from a healthy, varied, balanced diet. Other health professionals argue that with the different stresses of our modern environment we need extra supplementation, particularly the B group vitamins.

When brain and nerve cells send messages between themselves and throughout the body they rely on neurotransmitters. These are chemicals that transmit the body's signals. It is scientific fact that the B group vitamins are essential for the normal function of the brain, nerves and neurotransmitters. For example, it is the combination of vitamin B_5 (pantothenic acid) and choline, which produces acetylcholine, one of the major neurotransmitters.

So the argument is simple. Our micronutrients are depleted during stress. The more stress, the more depletion. So if you are suffering chronic stress, a B group supplement may improve your ability to cope with

B vitamins are essential for the normal function of the nerves and brain.

stress on a long term basis. Although the scientific evidence behind this argument is not strong, we do know that taking B group vitamins for stress will do you no harm.

Cancer

Although the true cause of cancer is unknown, we do know cancer cells are deranged cells that do not follow the normal rules of metabolism and cell division. Cancer cells set their own rules, showing no respect for the normal barriers and boundaries of organs. Cancer cells have their own excessive metabolism, hungrily stealing nutrients from normal cells.

What makes a cancer cell form in the first place is unknown, but we do know that there are many associations and known risk factors. The most obvious association is between cigarette smoke and cancer. There is no doubt cigarette smokers have a much higher risk for lung cancer than non–smokers. Interestingly, only 20% of smokers develop lung cancer. Science is not sure what prevents the other 80% from not developing lung cancer. Your genetic make–up is important but so are many other factors such as exposure to other environmental pollutants and toxins, life stresses and nutritional status. Unfortunately, many smokers are deluded into believing they can overcome the noxious effects of cigarettes by swallowing a vitamin supplement. Nothing could be further from the truth.

In the Nurses Health Study, around 87,000 nurses living in the Boston area were followed for over 15 years. Their health status was assessed including their diets, exercise habits, vitamin ingestion, smoking, hormone replacement and subsequent risk for major diseases. A recent paper released in the *Journal of the American Medical Association* suggested that in the group of nurses who had taken a multi–vitamin preparation

The B vitamins with folate help prevent cancer and heart disease.

with folic acid, there was no benefit in regards to cancer up to the 15 years point. Surprisingly, when the data was analysed for the 15 year and beyond mark, there was a 75% reduction in bowel cancer along with a reduction of breast cancer.

This study was not a blinded, controlled study but purely an observational trial which means there was not a placebo (or dummy pill) group against which to compare the vitamins. Also those taking vitamins tended to lead a healthier lifestyle. What this study does suggest is that vitamins taken over a long period show a clear benefit. Remember, vitamin therapy should be seen like superannuation. You pay now and reap the benefits later. There is certainly no evidence in any trial of harm from a multi–B with folic acid. At the worst you are blowing your money, but at the best you get a simple, relatively inexpensive treatment to reduce your risk for common cancers.

A recent study by CSIRO scientist Dr Michael Fenech showed that eating three times the recommended daily intake of folate and vitamin B_{12} may lower your risk for cancer and heart disease. Leafy green vegetables and grains are high in folate. Organ meats and fish are high in vitamin B_{12}. Dr Fenech suggests having these higher intakes of folate and vitamin B_{12} may slow the wear and tear of DNA. People with above average rates of DNA damage have two to three times the cancer risk compared with those with lower parameters of DNA damage.

DNA is the basic building block of the body. It is genetic

material that lives within the nucleus of the cells and determines all aspects of cellular function, including the cells ability to replicate. Cells, because of continuous functioning, wear out. As the DNA becomes damaged and breaks down, the wrong signals are sent out. The usual scenario is that those damaged cells are recognised by the defence or immune system and are broken down into their component parts and re–used. Some damaged cells, send the wrong genetic information and these are the cells that are thought to become cancerous.

Dr Fenech's research is vitally important in not only allowing us to understand the mechanisms of the generation of cancer, but also may suggest modes of prevention and treatment. Dr Fenech studied the levels of DNA damage in the chromosomes of a group of 1,000 South Australians. He found wide variations in the degree of damage amongst individuals in similar age groups. These differences may be due to:

◆ Genetic defects in the DNA repair mechanisms
◆ Exposure to carcinogens (cancer producing agents)
◆ Diets with excessive saturated fat and refined sugars
◆ Diets with varying levels of vitamins and minerals especially vitamin B_{12} and folate
◆ Other detrimental lifestyle factors which increase free radical exposure are pollution, cigarette smoking, excessive exercise, excessive emotional stress

Interestingly, Dr Fenech found a reduction of around 25% in chromosomal damage only in the group who had parameters of high DNA wear and tear. This reduction occurred after 12 weeks of supplementing their diet with folate and vitamin B_{12}. Those with parameters of minimal DNA wear and tear did not benefit from extra folate and vitamin B_{12}.

This is not surprising as you would only expect those at high risk to receive the true benefit. The problem, as with all supplementation, is deciding who is at high risk. If we had simple tests that could tell us which people are at high, intermediate and low risk, then all of our prevention programs could be targeted in a more cost effective manner.

I believe in the next ten years we will be able to attend a clinic and a sample (such as a buccal smear which scrapes a tiny layer of cells inside your mouth) will be able to map our genes and therefore our subsequent risk for future diseases.

The scenario goes something like this. Bill Jenner is 25 years old and wishes to know his lifelong risk. He attends his local 'genetic clinic' and has his buccal smear. Within 10 minutes he has a full genetic map.

- ◆ Heart Disease risk   85%
- ◆ Cancer risk
  - – Colon   15%
  - – Prostate   35%
  - – Lung   55%
  - – Liver damage   20%

With this very high risk for heart disease and lung cancer, Bill knows he should stop smoking immediately. His doctor can suggest a lifestyle program that includes appropriate dietary, exercise and quit smoking suggestions. Targeted therapy including appropriate vitamin, mineral and antioxidant treatment can ensure Bill enjoys a long and healthy life. Although this approach is not available at present, it is not far away – watch this space!

Heart disease

Over the past 30 years evidence is accumulating in relation to the B group vitamins, folic acid and heart disease. In the 1970s Professor David Wilcken and his research team at the University of NSW, suggested a link between an amino acid homocysteine (HC) and heart disease. Professor Wilcken found that people presenting with heart attacks or angina before the age of 55, often had much higher levels of homocysteine than people of a similar age without heart disease.

Numerous studies throughout the world since have confirmed this link. Homocysteine is a toxic amino acid that basically erodes the lining of the blood vessels thereby facilitating the passage of fat into the arteries. Homocysteine

also attacks the sticky cells in your bloodstream called platelets. These platelets work with your clotting factors to form clots at the site of damage. If they are not working properly you bleed excessively. If, however, they are made 'more sticky' by substances such as homocysteine, you clot excessively and are therefore more prone to conditions such as heart attack, angina and stroke.

Around 10% of the people in our society have elevated levels of homocysteine, basically due to a combination of diets high in methionine (from meats and eggs) and a defect usually in folic acid metabolism.

Once your homocysteine levels rise above 10 mmols/L, your risk for vascular disease starts. Like cholesterol, the higher the level, the higher the risk. Homocysteine is not routinely measured which I believe is a pity.

The beauty of the homocysteine story is the simplicity of treatment. The simple addition, in supplement form, of folic acid, vitamin B_{12} and vitamin B_6 can reduce homocysteine levels back to normal, in most cases. The usual dose of folic acid is 400 mcg daily. Most good vitamin B/folic acid combinations have this level along with appropriate vitamin B_{12} and vitamin B_6 doses. Again, as measurement of homocysteine is not standard, most people will benefit from adding a vitamin B with folic acid supplement to their daily regimen.

The B vitamins with folate aid in the prevention of cancer and heart disease. They can also play a part in a stress management regimen. Individually the B vitamins have more specific effects in higher doses, well in excess of the recommended daily allowances.

Vitamin B_1

Vitamin B_1 or thiamin is suggested to be an excellent supplement for people with alcohol problems. I am not suggesting if you drink to excess you should continue to do so and feel comforted by the fact you are taking vitamin B_1. I am merely suggesting that alcohol severely depletes vitamin B_1 levels and therefore this supplement may be of benefit, especially if you are trying to recover from the ravages of alcoholism. Vitamin B_1 also has been shown in some studies to improve memory. The suggested dose for both of these conditions is 100 mgs daily.

Vitamin B_2

Vitamin B_2 or riboflavin has been shown in a few trials to be useful in the prevention of migraine. Migraine can be a debilitating condition. Many of the medicinal agents used to treat this condition can have numerous acute and chronic side effects. As migraine can plague an individual for many years, the least toxic substances ingested the better. My advice is to try riboflavin in a dose of 400 mgs per day. It can't hurt and certainly may reduce the amount of episodes you suffer.

Carpal Tunnel Syndrome is a painful condition that affects the median nerve, the main nerve supply to the hand. The usual treatment is either an injection of cortisone into the nerve sheath or an operation that releases the nerve. Operations may be very successful, but obviously more drastic. Some people have found benefit from a combination of vitamin B_2 – 400 mgs daily and varying doses of vitamin B_6 of around 100 mgs daily. It is certainly worth a trial of this combination, before moving to the more invasive methods of treatment.

Vitamin B_3

One of the oldest methods of lowering cholesterol is using mega doses of vitamin B_3, otherwise known as niacin or nicotinic acid. Vitamin B_3 is not usually used to lower cholesterol these days because of a very effective group of agents known as the statins. Because of the powerful ability of these drugs in lowering cholesterol, many people have been lulled into a false sense of security about diet. They (falsely) believe that they can eat poorly and swallow an extra statin drug and this approach will protect them.

Vitamin B_3 significantly reduces LDL cholesterol.

This 'magic bullet' concept is just not true without a lifestyle change.

Vitamin B_3 is also not commonly used because of its significant side effect profile. Although it does not have any nasty long term side effects, its acute effects are dramatic. If you swallow Vitamin B_3 on an empty stomach (in the high doses necessary), you will flush like you've never flushed before. It is basically like having someone run a blow torch up your back.

The flushing effects can be minimised in most people by starting at low doses taken right in the middle of a meal, gradually increasing to the desired doses over a few months. The drug must be taken in divided doses (two to three times per day), commencing at 250 mgs gradually increasing to doses between 1 gm and 4 gm daily, depending on the cholesterol response.

I know what you're thinking! You're saying, why bother with

such a hassle of a program when you can swallow a powerful drug like a statin with minimal side effects? The reason to bother is as follows. Statins, although very powerful at lowering total cholesterol levels, have relatively weak effects at lowering triglycerides and elevating the good HDL cholesterol. Probably even more importantly, they have shown minimal benefit in reducing the most dangerous component of cholesterol, small, dense LDL. LDL is the bad cholesterol but it is basically the small, dense component that causes the mischief. This is the part of LDL that is easily oxidised by those nasty little devils, the free radicals. It is this oxidised, small, dense LDL cholesterol that crosses the blood vessel wall and forms the atherosclerotic plaque setting up the potential for plaque rupture and subsequent heart attack, unstable angina or its worst complication sudden cardiac death.

Vitamin B_3 has been shown to significantly reduce small dense LDL cholesterol. One of the tricks of cholesterol and lipid problems that has fooled the public, and unfortunately many doctors, is the misconception that a drop in cholesterol is always beneficial to the patient.

Although, on the whole, this is true, it is not always the case. Let me demonstrate this principle with two instructive cases. Peter Nolan is 48 years old. He suffered a minor heart attack at 46. Because of his young age an angiogram was performed showing a total block in his right coronary artery in the mid portion, a 40% block in a branch of his circumflex and a 20% block in the major left anterior descending artery.

His cardiologist immediately commenced him on a statin, aspirin and a drug known as a beta–blocker. At that stage his lipid profile was:

◆ Total Cholesterol
   6.4 mmol/L (normal range < 5 mmol/L)
◆ Triglycerides
   2.8 mmol/L (normal range < 1.5 mmol/L)
◆ HDL cholesterol
   0.9 mmol/L (normal range >1 mmol/L)

He commenced a low fat diet and initially lost 4 kilograms and felt very well. After a few months when the terror had worn off and the stresses from his job and family life re–emerged, he slackened off his diet and his cardiologist continued to push the statins. He asked his doctor about vitamin supplementation and was reassured he would obtain all the vitamins he needed from a healthy diet.

Despite some weight gain, his lipid profile remained seemingly excellent with the high dose of a statin.

◆ Total cholesterol   4.5 mmol/L
◆ Triglycerides   2 mmol/L
◆ HDL cholesterol   1.1 mmol/L

Six months later, he began to experience chest tightness when walking up a hill. These were the first symptoms he experienced since his initial heart attack. His cardiologist performed a stress test, which was abnormal, and he suggested a repeat angiogram. This revealed significant new blockages in his left anterior descending and circumflex with progression of his existing blockages.

The reason for this is that Peter has what is known as the dyslipidaemic profile. This fat or lipid profile in his bloodstream is probably significantly responsible for around 50% of the cases of coronary artery disease. The dyslipidaemic profile is due to an excess of small, dense LDL cholesterol. When LDL cholesterol is measured, it is not broken down into small, dense LDL or its more benign partner large, buoyant LDL. When statins are used, they have a powerful effect in lowering total LDL. Therefore you and your doctor are lulled into this false sense of security when you see your cholesterol plummeting but, unfortunately, not much is happening in the small, dense department. Therefore the fat is still pouring into your arteries despite the fact you think things are nice and stable.

Case two provides an interesting twist. Mario Gallo is 56 years old. He has just suffered an episode of unstable angina pectoris and was found on routine cholesterol testing to have the following profile.

- Total cholesterol   − 7.1 mmol/L
- Triglycerides   − 5.4 mmol/L
- HDL cholesterol   − 0.8 mmol/L

His astute cardiologist realised the statins are not effective alone in this setting, so he commenced a drug known as gemfibrozil. He returned to his family physician and didn't bother to attend his cardiologist for follow up. His repeat cholesterol levels were as follows after one month of treatment with gemfibrozil and a Mediterranean diet.

- Total cholesterol   7.5 mmol/L
- Triglycerides   1.3 mmol/L
- HDL cholesterol   1.6 mmol/L

His family physician and the patient were very disappointed by these results, so the gemfibrozil was stopped and replaced with a statin. Within one month his results were:

- Total cholesterol   5.4 mmol/L (down)
- Triglycerides   4.6 mmol/L (up)
- HDL cholesterol   1.0 mmol/L

With his tail between his legs, he returned to his cardiologist, to whom the explanation was obvious.

The gemfibrozil and the diet in combination had normalised his dyslipidaemic profile. The initial rise in his total cholesterol was due to a rise in his large, buoyant LDL (harmless rise of no significance). The marked drop in his triglycerides and accompanying rise in HDL suggest indirectly a drop in the bad small, dense LDL, which is exactly the desired change.

The family physician's inability to recognise this change led to the statin being introduced and the subsequent abnormalities seen on the blood tests.

In the 1980s, a researcher in Seattle, Dr Greg Brown released the results of the Familial Atherosclerosis Therapy Study (FATS) trial. This took people with cholesterol problems and proven atherosclerosis on a coronary angiogram and put them on varying doses and combinations of cholesterol lowering agents.

The 'holy grail' of cardiology is reversal of coronary artery disease, which is a possibility with the right approach. There have been a number of 'regression or reversal' trials with the FATS trial being the most famous.

Dr Brown and his co–workers found the best regression over a five year period was seen in people who were on combination therapy. The most effective combination was using vitamin B_3 (nicotinic acid) and a statin. This combination basically covers all bases. Small, dense LDL is not routinely measured so you will miss these people in 50% of heart disease cases. Dr Brown followed 70 men in his trial for ten years who elected to stay on combination therapy. In a group of people with stable heart disease on standard therapy, there should be a 2% mortality or death rate per year. This means in Dr Brown's group, 14 out of 70 should have been dead at the end of ten years.

The astounding fact is that in the group on combination therapy there were no deaths at the end of ten years, only one person out of 70 had suffered a minor heart attack. Apart from this trial, these statistics are unheard of in cardiology. Well, you may ask, why isn't everybody with a heart problem on combination therapy?

Taking vitamin B_3 requires a big effort on the part of the patient. It does have annoying side effects and around 10% of people cannot tolerate the drug, no matter how carefully they follow the low dose, slow build up, take it in the middle of a meal approach.

Also it does take an effort to remember to swallow the pill 2 to 3 times per day right in the middle of a meal. In our push button society, it is so much easier to take the quick fix statins. There is no doubt from all the trials that statins do reduce your risk by around 30%, which is good but not great. Recent work has shown a 90% reduction in cardiac events (such as heart attack or sudden death) with lifestyle modification, combination cholesterol lowering treatment (statin and nicotinic acid) and antioxidant therapy.

The combination of a statin and nicotinic acid has a much greater effect than this and (I believe) fortunately we are seeing a resurgence in nicotinic acid use. This is especially so with the newer forms of niacin. In the past, scientists played with different forms of slow release nicotinic acid. Unfortunately, these older, slow release forms induced liver disease in a significant proportion of people taking the drug.

Recently a new form of nicotinic acid has emerged. This slow release form combines niacin with inositol (a form of carbohydrate) which markedly reduces the flushing but is still very effective. Hopefully with this new drug, nicotinic acid, will regain its place as a very safe, effective form of cholesterol lowering, especially used in combination with the statins.

A major advantage of nicotinic acid is its ability to not only lower small, dense LDL cholesterol but it also has a marked effect on lowering triglycerides (20 to 40%) and increasing HDL cholesterol (15 to 30%). Another advantage of nicotinic acid is its ability to lower Lp(a). No other medication, apart from oestrogen, can lower Lp(a).

Lp(a) is responsible for as much as 30% of coronary artery disease.

Lp(a) is primarily responsible for as much as 30% of the cases of coronary artery disease and to date there is no specific therapy to target Lp(a) apart from nicotinic acid. With increasing awareness of this common genetic abnormality, early preventative assessment and treatment may well significantly reduce the impact of Lp(a).

Vitamin B$_6$

Vitamin B$_6$ has been shown in some studies to lessen the effects of the pre–menstrual syndrome (PMS). Although PMS is not a disease state, and is obviously related to subtle hormonal aberrations in combination with other life factors, it can still be a debilitating condition for many women (not to mention their partners and family). The recommended doses vary between 5 to 200 mgs per day (depending on which expert you believe), starting on day ten of the menstrual cycle, continuing until day three of the following cycle.

As already mentioned when discussing vitamin B_2, vitamin B_6 is worth considering in combination with vitamin B_2 for treatment of Carpal Tunnel Syndrome. Again, vitamin B_6, in combination with folic acid and vitamin B_{12}, lower homocysteine levels which have been directly linked to an increased incidence of premature vascular disease. Doses above 250 mgs daily should be avoided.

Vitamin B_5

Vitamin B_5 or pantothenic acid has been shown to be a useful adjunct to cholesterol lowering therapy. Doses of around 900 mgs daily significantly lowered cholesterol and improved the cholesterol to HDL ratio.

Folic acid

Folic acid in doses of 400 mcg per day or greater has been shown to have a myriad of benefits. The cardiovascular homocysteine effect has been well demonstrated from numerous studies. The effects on improving mood and lifting depression are becoming more recognised. Folic acid has a major preventative effect on neural tube defects which lead to spina bifida and related disorders. Folic acid's place in cancer prevention is also being well established. Finally, folic acid is an integral part of the formation of red blood cells and is used to treat certain types of anaemia. Basically, folic acid is an all–round good guy that is important for good health.

Vitamin B_{12}

There is a common condition known as pernicious anaemia that usually affects the older age group. This is an immune based condition where the body recognises part of the stomach cells as being foreign. An antibody is made which stops this important chemical from being produced by the stomach. This antibody binds to vitamin B_{12} allowing it to be delivered into the blood–stream towards the end of the small bowel.

In pernicious anaemia, vitamin B_{12} is not absorbed, and affected people become very weak from anaemia and can also become dizzy from spinal cord problems. If this condition is not detected and is treated with regular injections of vitamin B_{12}, permanent damage to the spinal cord may occur. Oral vitamin B_{12} is of no use in this condition. Taking oral folic acid with untreated pernicious anaemia may deplete vitamin B_{12} stores even further, thereby worsening the condition. Especially in elderly people, taking a B group supplement with folic acid as a 'tonic' cannot be recommended, as it may mask pernicious anaemia.

Overall, I believe there is strong evidence in support of regular supplementation with a multivitamin B along with folic acid. To B or not to B, the answer is yes.

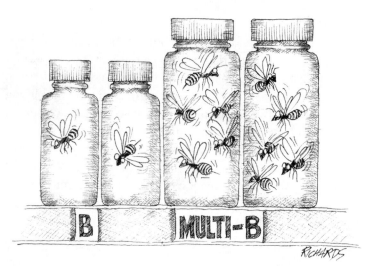

CHAPTER NINE

DINING FOR MINERALS

If you believe all the hype, we bipedal, carbon–based life forms who comprise the species known affectionately as homo sapiens, should consider ourselves more special than all other life forms. Spiritual matters aside, we are in reality just the top of the food chain and, apart from some major rearrangements in DNA, our bodies are made from the same basic building blocks as all other life forms.

Minerals are a vital component of all these life forms. Minerals are not manufactured in the body and must be derived from either food or supplements. Without the recommended daily allowance of all the different types of minerals, we may develop some form of deficiency.

An example is osteoporosis. There are many predisposing and causative factors in osteoporosis apart from a lack of calcium in the diet. Prolonged immobilisation due to disease states, such as an overactive thyroid or adrenal gland or failing ovaries, can also play a role. It is estimated that the average calcium intake in our diets is somewhere between 500 to 700 mgs per day, which is two–thirds the recommended daily intake. Another alarming fact is that the average calcium intake of a teenage female is similar to that suggested for a five year old.

It is no wonder that by the time teenage females reach middle age, their bones are already screaming out for calcium. Many post–menopausal women consume calcium supplements but this is shutting the gate after the horse has bolted. The fact that osteoporosis is so common in our society is a strong pointer in support of the 'subtle nutritional deficiency' argument that, for the most part, is rejected by the medical and nutritional profession.

We should obtain all the nutrients we need from a balanced diet. This balanced diet, doesn't appear to exist. Results from an American study known as the United States National Health and Nutrition Examination Survey (NHANES II) found that 25% of total calories come from sugar and 34% from fat. This implies that over 50% of our calories come from foods with poor nutritional value. Further information tells us that around 50% of people living in Western society don't consume fruit or juice on any particular day. Twenty percent of people rarely eat vegetables on a daily basis. Less than 10% of people consume the recommended five or more daily servings of fruit and vegetables.

These statistics go on and on, suggesting that the health messages regarding a balanced diet do not really reach and affect eating habits. So many people don't eat properly. Unfortunately, with our society being increasingly geared toward comfort and the quick fix, people are not putting in the long term effort for their own bodies. One day they end up in either a coronary care unit, a cancer ward or having orthopaedic surgery for an osteoporotic fracture due to the lack of effort in their younger days. They expect some pill or operation to cure their ills.

Calcium

Ninety percent of the calcium in our bodies exists in our bones and teeth, but there is still an abundant amount of calcium found in every cell in our body. Calcium is vital for muscle contraction, clotting and the generation of nerve impulses. Therefore changes in total body calcium affects more than the bones. Calcium deficiency cannot be measured in the blood with any degree of accuracy because of the amount in the bones. The blood will always draw on the bone stores long before it allows the blood levels to drop. Low blood calcium levels are usually due to abnormalities in the hormones and vitamins that control calcium metabolism, such as parathormone and vitamin D.

I believe it is important to try your best to eat a balanced diet and in regard to osteoporosis, supplement much earlier than when a diagnosis of osteoporosis is made. Although osteoporosis is the major condition associated with lack of calcium, there are also strong associations with high blood pressure and muscle cramps.

My opinion regarding calcium intake is that the recommended daily allowance for calcium is too low. I would suggest a daily intake of somewhere between 1500 to 2500 mgs from both food and supplementation. Supplementation above this level has been shown to contribute to kidney stones and kidney dysfunction in predisposed people.

Problems with excess calcium intake are also compounded by accompanying excess intake of Vitamin D. Vitamin D acts by increasing the absorption of calcium and affecting its kidney excretion. One interesting concept from the Male Health Professionals' Study, which surveyed 50,000 doctors, suggested a higher rate of prostate cancer in those who had an excessive intake of calcium from food and supplements.

It gets back to that very important theme throughout my books – balance. It is vital to take the right dose. When we think of minerals it is easy to focus on calcium, but there are 20 other minerals all in their own way, essential to our health and well–being. In fact, in isolation calcium is somewhat ineffective in

Calcium in the bones is good. Calcium in the coronary arteries is an indication of the build up of fatty plaque, which is not good.

performing its ubiquitous functions and certainly needs at least the recommended daily allowance of many of the other minerals.

Calcium, magnesium, phosphorous and fluoride all work in concert with many other chemicals and lesser known minerals to maintain the integrity of our bones and joints. Although all the minerals deserve greater attention, I would refer you to a more in–depth publication if you required the intricate function and uses for the other less publicised minerals. Suffice to say, most of the multivitamin supplements on the market contain a correct blend of these minerals along with the B group vitamins and often other important chemical constituents.

Sodium

Sodium is a common mineral that is also called an electrolyte. Although the suggested daily intake of salt is somewhere between 1,000 to 2,000 mgs, many people in Western society consume between 2 to 5 times this amount. When you think of excessive salt intake, think of high blood pressure.

There is a link between high blood pressure and communities with a life long high salt intake. Salt induced changes in blood pressure do not affect all individuals and some recent work suggests some people may even benefit from having higher salt intakes. It has been shown that around one third of the general population and half of people with high blood pressure are sensitive to the effects of salt.

If you take people with a salt metabolism problem and expose them to high salt levels in their diets, they will probably develop high blood pressure with its subsequent vicious complications. As with everything in life, the risks and benefits need to be balanced. I have some very practical and simple advice. If you already have established high blood pressure or a strong family history of high blood pressure, I would consume a low salt diet.

Five Day Salt Test

If you want to test your own salt sensitivity, consume your usual diet for five days. Rent a blood pressure machine and measure your blood pressure four times a day during this time. Then for five days follow a very rigid salt restriction

1. No salt on table
2. No salt in cooking
3. Avoid obvious salty foods

Salty foods include all take away food. You would also need to avoid processed, packaged foods. Products such as peanut butter, Vegemite, tomato sauce, margarine, cheese, organ meats and mineral water can have a high salt content. During the last two days of this restricted diet, re–measure your blood pressure four times a day. If your blood pressure has dropped by greater than 5 mm Hg systolic and diastolic, then you are probably salt sensitive and would benefit from ongoing salt restriction.

If you remove a person at birth from Western society and put them into a society where there is little salt, minimal stress and no motorised transport, it is unlikely this person will ever develop high blood pressure regardless of their genetics.

Salt should be restricted in the following instances:

1. Established high blood pressure (BP)
2. Strong family history of high BP
3. Heart failure
4. Kidney failure
5. Other states of fluid retention

For those of us who do not fit into this category, I would not suggest we use salt in the same way a particular Russian president enjoyed alcohol, but there is also no real indication for salt restriction.

Potassium

Another major electrolyte is potassium. The body contains around 90 gms of sodium and most of this is outside the cells. There are around 140 gms of potassium in the body, most of which are inside the cells. Sodium and potassium act together to create an electrical balance between the inside and the outside of the cells. There needs to be a balance between sodium and potassium.

Although the body is geared beautifully for balance, and will attempt its best to maintain the normal intra and extra cellular relationship between sodium and potassium, many illnesses can disrupt this balance.

Taking excessive salt can overload the outside of cells, water–logging the extra–cellular space. Anywhere in the body there is sodium, water follows. Lack or excess potassium can be even more dramatic. A progressive loss of potassium through fluid loss, kidney disease or drug therapy can lead to weakness, cardiac rhythm disturbances, kidney abnormalities and a rise in blood pressure.

Bill is 65 years old. He had coronary artery bypass surgery two years previously which was complicated by acute kidney failure. He had suffered a heart attack when he was 63 following 15 years of high blood pressure. He had been taking a diuretic (fluid tablet) for ten years but had not been advised to restrict his salt intake.

He presented to the local emergency department following a collapse at home. On arrival his electrocardiogram (heart rhythm trace) was abnormal showing frequent ectopic beats. The attending doctor collected blood for routine testing and to exclude a heart attack. Bill's blood potassium was 2.8 mmol/L (normal is 3.5 to 5 mmol/L) and it was felt this was the likely cause for his collapse. His magnesium levels were also low.

On further testing with a cardiac ultrasound it was found that his heart function was impaired, necessitating a marked change in his drug therapy. With improved treatment for his heart problem and proper potassium and magnesium replacement therapy, his condition significantly improved and he had no further collapses.

No matter how healthy or how unwell you may be, you can become very unhealthy or exacerbate your underlying condition by not having the proper balance of electrolytes.

There are many foods that contain potassium and magnesium and although there is no justification for routine supplementation in healthy people, it is vital that a normal balance is maintained, especially in acute situations like that experienced by Bill. So often people are prescribed diuretic or fluid therapy without adequate potassium or magnesium replacement therapy.

Despite the advances in the treatment of heart disease, around one in four people in Western society will die from a heart attack. When a heart attack occurs, one in three of its victims will die suddenly. The blocked artery causes a lack of oxygen to the heart muscle that induces electrical instability. This irritated heart then goes into a rhythm known as ventricular fibrillation, which is a quivering of the heart muscle. The heart ceases to pump and the person collapses.

Numerous studies have shown disturbances in potassium and magnesium are very common in people who die suddenly following a heart attack. This is a further pointer to the argument that many seemingly healthy members of our society are nutritionally deficient. I am talking about vitamin and mineral deficiency, not a deficiency of the macronutrients fat, protein and carbohydrate. They cruise along undetected until something goes wrong, such as a heart attack, which unmasks their electrolyte disturbance, further irritates their already irritated heart and down they go in a screaming heap.

Copper

When we think of copper, we think of copper pipes used in plumbing. This isn't a bad analogy because copper is a vital chemical for many reactions in the body, in particular the integrity of our blood vessels. Blood vessels that rupture, especially large vessels such as the aorta, often lack adequate amounts of copper. Some quarters in complementary medicine also believe that subtle copper deficiency can also contribute to your hair going grey. I must state that I felt age also had something to do with this.

Zinc

Zinc and copper work together to enhance the action of one of the body's most important endogenous (or internal) antioxidants. This substance is known as superoxide dismutase (SOD). Without this enzyme functioning normally, the body will become quickly overwhelmed by free radicals. Zinc has been shown to have a place in the treatment of sexual dysfunction and prostate problems. It also plays an important role in hair and skin condition. A recent use for zinc is in combination with vitamin C and echinacea in the treatment and prevention of colds and flu. Like most medical treatments, some studies in this area have been very promising but others have shown little benefit.

Chromium and non–insulin dependant diabetes

An interesting trace metal, which is gaining supplemental prominence, is chromium. Chromium is being suggested in some circles as an adjunct to weight loss but I must stress, the data is very weak and limited. I believe the greatest promise for chromium is in the area of glucose metabolism.

Later onset or better described as non–insulin dependent diabetes is a very common condition. As a dietary pattern in any community changes to contain high amounts of saturated fats and refined sugars, the rates of non–insulin dependent diabetes mellitus (NIDDM) climb rapidly. Although NIDDM is a disease precipitated by Western society, it is based around the presence of a specific gene known as the gene for insulin resistance.

Anyone with a rudimentary knowledge of diabetes would suggest it is a disorder relating to sugar intake, beginning in the pancreas (a large gland that rests on the front of the spine, squirting digestive enzymes into the gut and also making insulin and other hormones). Pancreatic failure is mainly responsible for insulin dependent diabetes (a disorder usually starting in young children) but not for non–insulin dependent diabetes (emerging in mid life). Non–insulin dependent diabetes starts at the level of the cells.

Imagine your cells to be like shops along a road. The road is like the blood vessels. Different delivery men (usually proteins in the body) deliver supplies to the shops (Nutrients delivered to the cells). Major nutrients or macronutrients like fat, protein and carbohydrates need to be delivered into the cells in a regulated fashion to prevent the cells overloading. These substances are used as fuel to drive the cells and other functions such as replenishing the enzyme systems. The entry of these substances, especially glucose, is regulated by insulin. If you are insulin resistant then glucose, and to a lesser extent fat and protein, do not enter the cell as readily, staying outside the cell in the blood vessel or within the surrounding supporting or connective tissue.

Eventually these substances spill over into fat cells and into the blood vessel wall. One of the body's major responses to this is to release more insulin. This does allow more sugar to enter the cells, but insulin itself can increase fat deposition and alter fat metabolism.

This insulin resistance syndrome predisposes you to five main problems:

1. Tendency to non–insulin dependent diabetes
2. Tendency to high blood pressure
3. Tendency to cholesterol abnormalities
4. Tendency to obesity
5. Tendency to atherosclerosis

Around 30% of Caucasians and 100% of black races possess the gene for insulin resistance (IR). The best prevention of the IR gene manifesting and causing its big five problems, is to avoid a diet high in saturated fat and refined sugars, and maintain a regular exercise and movement program.

An added helpful supplement, in regard to preventing diabetes, is to take daily between 200 to 500 mcgs of chromium. At the same time, each day on your cereal, add 1 teaspoon of cinnamon powder. Both these substances, when combined, have been shown to improve insulin resistance (based on preliminary trials that at this stage give results that are promising, but not conclusive).

Selenium

Finally another mineral, selenium, although controversial, is gaining more acceptance. Selenium is found in brazil nuts, organ meats, seafoods, cereals and vegetables like broccoli and celery. It has been shown to reduce the risk of heart disease and cancer in selected populations. Some studies have shown similar benefit with selenium supplementation in reducing common cancers, and a few studies have shown a trend towards a reduction in fatal and non–fatal heart attack.

One of the problems with making supplementation recommendations is the variable amount of selenium in the soil. In certain countries such as parts of China, the soil is so deficient in selenium that there is a high rate of Keshan's disease, which is a severe cardiomyopathy (cardiac muscle weakness), caused by selenium deficiency. Selenium supplementation has been beneficial in some countries in treating asthma, arthritis and cataracts.

Although the recommended daily intake of selenium is only 50 to 70 mcg, the cancer prevention doses have been between 100 to 200 mcg per day. Toxicity has been reported in daily intakes greater than 600 mcg.

Selenium enhances the action of vitamins E, C and beta–carotene. In some countries such as Australia, the food regulatory bodies make it difficult to obtain selenium in supplement form, whereas it is freely available in other countries.

Total mineral package

Nature is clever and has blended minerals into a few common and essential foods. We all know the most common source of calcium is dairy products. There are now excellent low fat milks with high calcium content along with other essential minerals. For all the other minerals, I would suggest eating a diet high in the following foods:

1. Wholegrain foods – breads, cereals
2. Nuts and legumes
3. Avocado
4. Leafy green vegetables
5. Seafood

With the change in all aspects of food cultivation, processing and delivery to the consumer, there has been a definite reduction in the amount of vitamins and minerals in our processed foods. Therefore it is my recommendation to supplement with a general multi–vitamin and mineral combination. Remember, no supplement is an alternative to a balanced diet and healthy lifestyle.

Sources of minerals and trace elements and their uses

Calcium

Function Growth and maintenance of healthy teeth and bones; nerve function; blood clotting; muscle contraction; metabolises iron.

Sources Fish (especially those eaten with bones); soybeans; dairy products; almonds; sesame seeds; sunflower seeds; watercress; fortified cereals. Vitamin D facilitates uptake.

Effects of deficiency or excess Deficiency can cause rickets, osteomalacia, osteoporosis.

Chromium (trace element)

Function Functioning of skeletal muscles; storing and metabolising sugars and fats.

Sources Unrefined wholegrain and cereal products; fish and shellfish; brewers yeast; beef.

Effects of deficiency or excess Deficiency can cause depression, confusion, irritability. Excess can be toxic.

Cobalt (trace element)

Function Component of vitamin B12 which prevents anaemia.

Sources Meat; liver; kidney; shellfish; green leafy vegetables.

Effects of deficiency or excess Deficiency causes lack of vitamin B12, leading to pernicious anaemia; bowel disorders; weak muscles.

Copper (trace element)

Function Formation of red blood cells; growth of bones; absorption of iron; pigmentation of hair and skin.

Sources Shellfish; nuts; liver; kidney; pulses; brewers yeast; tap water from copper pipes.
Effects of deficiency or excess Deficiency can cause anaemia, low white blood cell count. Excess can be toxic.

Fluorine (trace element)

Function Strengthens teeth and bones.
Sources Fluoridated tap water and toothpastes; fish (especially those eaten with bones); meat; tea; cereals.
Effects of deficiency or excess Deficiency causes tooth decay, osteoporosis. Excess causes mottled and discoloured teeth, increased density of bones in the spine, pelvis and limbs and calcified ligaments.

Iodine (trace element)

Function Production of hormones in the thyroid gland which control metabolism; promotes growth; promotes energy; mental alertness
Sources Iodised salt; Irish moss; kelp; seafood; fruit and vegetables grown in soils containing iodine.
Effects of deficiency or excess Deficiency causes goitre, weight gain, lack of energy. Excess can cause thyroid diseases.

Iron

Function Production of haemoglobin; distribution of oxygen and removal of carbon dioxide in body tissues; production of myoglobin (red pigment in muscles).
Sources Red meat; liver; kidney; oysters; kelp; pulses; dried fruits; nuts; oats.
Effects of deficiency or excess Deficiency causes anaemia.

Magnesium

Function Healthy teeth and bones; functioning of the nerves, muscles and metabolic enzymes.

Sources Wholewheat cereals and products; eggs; meat; nuts; pulses; seeds.

Effects of deficiency or excess Deficiency causes muscle cramps, tremors, tics, loss of appetite, nausea, insomnia, irregular heart beat.

Manganese (trace element)

Function Functioning of the nerves, muscles and many enzymes; bone strength.

Sources Whole grains; nuts; pulses; avocado; egg yolk; green leafy vegetables.

Effects of deficiency or excess Deficiency can cause bone deformities and impede growth rate.

Molybdenum (trace element)

Function Metabolism of iron; male sexual function; prevention of dental caries

Sources Oats; barley; pulses; root vegetables; liver.

Effects of deficiency or excess Excess can prevent body from utilising copper.

Phosphorus

Function Conversion and storage of energy; healthy bones; function of muscles, nerves and some enzymes; intestinal absorption of certain foods.

Sources Meat; poultry; fish and shellfish; nuts; seeds; pulses; dairy products; eggs.

Effects of deficiency or excess Deficiency causes bone pain;

stiff joints; disorders of the central nervous system; weakness. Excess can interfere with intestinal absorption of calcium, iron, magnesium and zinc.

Potassium

Function Maintains balance of fluids and pH in the body; disposal of body wastes; aids in sending oxygen to the brain; function of nerves and muscles.

Sources Fresh fruits and vegetables; whole grains and products; prunes; milk.

Effects of deficiency or excess Deficiency can case muscular weakness and paralysis, low blood pressure; thirst; loss of appetite; sensitivity to noise. Excess can aggravate some heart conditions.

Selenium (trace element)

Function Functioning of the red and white blood cells; along with Vitamin E works as an antioxidant; detoxifies metals including cadmium, mercury and lead; may protect against some cancers; prevents dandruff and some skin disorders; healthy liver function.

Sources Garlic; onions; whole wheat and products; fish and shellfish; red meat; chicken; broccoli; brewers yeast; Brazil nuts.

Effects of deficiency or excess Deficiency causes premature aging, cardiovascular disease and asthma and may be a factor in cancer. Excess can cause neurological disorders.

Sodium

Function Along with potassium maintains balance of fluids, especially water, and pH in the body; function of nerves and muscles.

Sources Common salt, baking powder; cured and smoked fish and meats; kelp; beets; artichokes; coconut; figs.

Effects of deficiency or excess Deficiency can cause heat prostration, dehydration, low blood pressure and indigestion.

Excess causes high blood pressure, heart disorders and oedema (fluid retention).

Sulphur (trace element)

Function Synthesis of protein; promotes healthy skin, hair and nails; combats bacterial infection.
Sources Meat; fish; dairy products; eggs; pulses; cabbage.
Effects of deficiency or excess Deficiency can cause skin diseases.

Zinc (trace element)

Function Formation of insulin in body; release of vitamin A; healing; healthy reproductive organs; functioning of growth and development enzymes.
Sources Red meat, liver; egg yolks; dairy products; whole wheat and products; oysters; brewers yeast..
Effects of deficiency or excess Deficiency can cause infertility, enlarged prostate gland, acne and skin disorders, slow healing of wounds, slow physical, mental and sexual development. Excess can cause nausea, diarrhoea, dizziness and dehydration.

CHAPTER TEN

PHYTONUTRIENTS

One of our worst childhood memories comes from those three words, 'Eat your vegetables!' I'm sorry my friends, but mother was right. Every time she made you sit at the table until the last carrot was finished, on each occasion when you couldn't watch television until all your peas were consumed, when she forced you (with the threat of some evil like the 'Boogie man') to down the last Brussels sprout (I still feel sick at the mention of that little number), mum was right. I am afraid to admit it but mother had an amazing insight into physiology and all things nutritious.

How do I know this to be true? The answer is simple. Numerous long term dietary trials and population studies have shown an unequivocal, inverse relationship between the consumption of fruits and vegetables and the incidence of heart disease and cancer, Western society's two biggest killers. The daily consumption of two to three pieces of fruit along with a wide variety of vegetables (up to five serves) can help prevent these two common killers.

Fruit and vegetables contain a ubiquitous group of substances with the extraordinary name of phytonutrients. This basically means 'plant foods or nutrients'. These phytonutrients are beneficial to the plant itself as well as to us when we eat them. To use the example of an orange: there are around 200 distinct phytochemicals which give an orange its flavour and texture as well as the ability to prevent viral, bacterial and fungal attack. These special nutrients also counter the free radical effect (oxidisation) and reduce the damaging effect of ultraviolet exposure from the sun. When we consume fruits and vegetables, we receive the protection and health benefits.

Studies from Greece and China have shown a 50% reduction in various types of cancers for those with high consumption levels of fruit and vegetable (Greece) and soy products

(China), compared to people with low intakes of these foods.

Types of phytonutrients

The five main groups of phytonutrients
1. Phytosterols
2. Glutathione
3. Carotenoids
4. Flavonoids
5. Terpenoids

Phytosterols

The big dietary news in 1999 was the release of the amazing new margarine that lowered cholesterol. Every sufferer or potential sufferer of heart disease rushed out to their local supermarket, fighting off all comers to purchase their tub of this 'wonder margarine'.

I am not denying or down playing the excellent benefits of these margarines that reduce your total cholesterol and your LDL (bad) cholesterol by around 10 to 15%, but nature knew about these phytosterols long before the scientists. The most common sterol is cholesterol. There are many different types of sterols, which compete for absorption in the gut. If you supplement with a different sterol, rather than swallowing too much cholesterol, your cholesterol has to compete with the other sterols and not as much is absorbed. Therefore, your cholesterol level drops.

The good news is that there is a significant amount of sterols in plants which block cholesterol absorption (there is no cholesterol in plants). These sterols are in most fruits and vegetables. An excellent source of plant sterols is the avocado. Avocados contain the good fats (monounsaturated fats), high levels of folic acid and significant amounts of phytosterols.

A colleague and friend, Professor David Colquhoun, is one of the world experts on the cardiac benefits of monounsaturated fats. He fed a group of people a half to a whole avocado per day for a month. This dropped their cholesterol levels and they also lost weight.

Glutathione

The sulphur compounds found in many plants are a major component of a substance known as glutathione. This is an important component of your body's internal antioxidant system, which works alongside the antioxidants you consume in your diet and supplement regimen. Glutathione is found in cabbage, garlic, onions, Brussels sprouts (mother are you listening) and vegetables such as broccoli and cauliflower.

Carotenoids

Altogether, there are around 600 specific types of carotenoids found in fruit and vegetables. The carotenoids are largely responsible for giving specific plants their colourings and they have many other amazing life preserving properties. There are five major carotenoid compounds. These and the foods that contain them are listed in the carotenoids and foods table.

One of the fascinating facts regarding carotenoid substances is that cooking improves the absorption. Another important and often overlooked point is the importance of vitamin E along with protein and dietary fat which all increase the absorption of the carotenoids.

Carotenoid actions

Vitamin A formation
Vitamin A is a fat soluble vitamin, vital for many cellular reactions especially involving the immune system and the skin.

Antioxidants
Carotenoids have strong antioxidant properties. It is felt that they contribute strongly to the marked reduction in many common degenerative diseases among people who consume significant amounts of fruit and vegetables. High consumption of carotenoids are thought to reduce:

- ◆ Premature aging
- ◆ Cancer
- ◆ Atherosclerosis

Carotenoids and Foods

◆ Alpha and beta–carotene
  – Carrots
  – Pumpkins
  – Apricots
  – Cantaloupe
  – Leafy green vegetables
  – Sweet potato
  – Winter squash
◆ Lutein
  – Leafy green vegetables
  – Pumpkins
  – Red peppers
◆ Zeanthin
  – Mangoes
  – Nectarines
  – Oranges, Mandarins, Tangerines
  – Papaya
  – Peaches
◆ Cryptoanthin
  – Mangoes
  – Nectarines
  – Oranges, Mandarins, Tangerines
  – Papaya
  – Peaches
◆ Lycopene
  – Cooked tomato
  – Tomato sauce
  – Tomato paste
  – Guava
  – Pink grapefruit
  – Watermelon

♦ Eye diseases – cataracts, macular degeneration
♦ Other degenerative diseases, for example dementia

Boost immunity

The immune or defence system of your body requires the total package of micronutrients for efficient functioning. Carotenoids provide many of these vital biochemical components.

Vision

Carotenoids offer special protection to the eyes. They are necessary for sharp and detailed vision and also filter blue light while preventing redness and damage from UV light.

Cellular communication

The body has an extraordinary system of communication. Each action, whether it be the gross movement of a limb or the production of a protein in the liver, is regulated down to the most minute detail. Each cell acts as a signaling outpost of the brain and the immune system, ensuring its own needs are served, so it (the cell) can then, in turn serve the needs of the entire body. These systems have been designed to ensure millisecond by millisecond communication both at a cell to cell level and throughout the body.

Flavonoids

There are five important flavonoids:

Proanthocyanidins

These are derived from either grape seed or pine bark extracts. They are now freely available in supplement form and although there are no long term placebo controlled clinical trials to support their use, numerous anecdotal case histories claim benefits from conditions as varied as heart disease, cancer, chronic fatigue syndrome, fibromyalgia and numerous immune diseases. Laboratory work has demonstrated these agents to be 20 times more potent than vitamin C and 50 times more potent than vitamin E.

Cellular communication and carotenoids

Communication throughout the body is through a coordinated set of mechanisms. Sometimes this may be through direct nervous impulses, sometimes through hormones, proteins and other substances (often in conjunction with the immune or defence system). These chemicals work together on a micro level, to ensure efficient cell to cell communication. On the surface of each cell is a set of receptors, which act as the intercom between the exterior and interior of the cell. Chemical transmitters lock into these receptors. The receptors then send messages into the cell or open the cells doorways (otherwise called channels) to allow different nutrients (eg glucose, fatty acids or amino acids) to enter the cell.

This cell to cell communication is vital. Unfortunately, with the extra toxins pouring into our systems from the varying sources of excessive saturated fat, pollution, cigarette smoke and the numerous food additives, colourings and preservatives, this intricate communication network often loses its efficiency. It is the carotenoid compounds that strengthen the growth regulatory signals between these cells.

Another promising aspect of cell to cell communication comes from the aloe vera plant. Aloe vera (which is not a carotenoid) is an excellent source of monosaccharides, which are forms of carbohydrates. These monosaccharides combine with proteins to form substances known as glycoproteins. These glyconutritionals are essential for normal cell to cell communication. DNA creates the messages, which form differing combinations of glycoproteins, depending on the necessary function the DNA is coding. For example, if the particular part of DNA is coded to produce insulin (the main regulator of glucose within cells), a certain series of messages will be sent by DNA to create a series of glycoproteins, which will eventually contribute to the production of insulin.

Personally I have seen numerous patients who have benefited from using supplements of proanthocyanidins. I recall one young woman who attended a lecture I was giving on the benefits of a healthy lifestyle along with antioxidant supplementation. After the lecture she approached me stating she had heard me speak before and wanted to thank me. From the age of 15 she had suffered fibromyalgia, which is a painful muscle condition. She had missed 12 months of schooling and was regularly using pain killers. She had been desperate for relief and after hearing me speak, felt she would try some grape seed extract. Amazingly, within a few weeks of commencing the extract, her pain had ceased and she returned to school.

Polyphenols
These are very strong antioxidants which are found in different sources such as extra virgin olive oil, tea and red wine. Numerous epidemiologic studies have suggested strong health benefits from regular consumption of one or more of these. Green tea has been known as a health drink for many years. From both Chinese and Japanese studies the link between drinking green tea and low rates of cancer has been suggested. One interesting study showed the area of Japan where most of the green tea is produced has lower rates of cancer compared with the rest of Japan.

Isoflavones
Soy beans contain phytoestrogens. It is fascinating that in premenopausal women with high oestrogen levels, the isoflavones in soy beans bind to oestrogen receptors, thereby blocking the effects of oestrogens. However, when, post–menopausal women lose their oestrogen, the isoflavones can act as a weaker version of oestrogen.

Using soy products may lower the chances of developing hormone related cancers such as breast and prostate. Regular consumption of soy has also shown to lower pre–menopausal symptoms and lessen osteoporosis. Soy products also benefit people with cholesterol abnormalities. A handful of studies have shown reduced total cholesterol levels in those given soy protein. One recent study showed a 28% increase in HDL cholesterol in those given isoflavones (40 mgs per day) derived from red clover.

Quercetin

This is one of the major antioxidants in red wine and is also available in supplement form for those who for any reason don't want to or can't consume red wine.

Citrus Bioflavonoids

Long before science was able to categorise all of these wonderful chemicals, the benefits of citrus fruits have been well established. The bioflavonoids are some of the many wonderful substances in citrus fruits that maintain good health.

Terpenoids

The terpenoids are found in grain foods. It is these substances that are felt to contribute to the cholesterol lowering properties of wheat, oats, rye, millet, rice, barley and other grains.

Phytonutrient conclusion

With modern science progressing in leaps and bounds, we are rapidly becoming able to extract most of the chemicals in plants and put them in some form of supplement. This may seem like a lazy approach but with our rapidly changing world, most of us can't keep up, let alone sit down to consume healthy meals three times a day. This may be the way of the future. A few inventive companies are now concentrating fruit and vegetable extracts into capsules or drinks with positive results.

One recent paper published in the *Journal of Integrative Medicine*, showed a significant improvement in all parameters of immune function in an older population, given a fruit and vegetable extract in capsule form, for an eight day period. Another study from *Nutrition Research* showed a highly significant reduction in the DNA damage in the white cells of 20 elderly volunteers who took these same supplements for the same time period. Some of the major companies producing supplements have realised the power of phytonutrients. Rather than using a synthetic source for their raw vitamins, they are deriving them from an organic source. Thus a range of phytonutrients are incorporated into their supplements. This allows the consumer the best of both worlds. They are taking the vitamin in doses that are higher than they could derive from food and they are receiving the benefits of the hundreds of phytochemicals that naturally occur in the plants.

Nobody suggests that consuming supplements should be seen as a replacement for a healthy lifestyle. It is an adjunct to sensible living. There is no doubt you will derive the greatest benefit from regular consumption of a variety of fruits and vegetables. You are probably now at the age when your mother doesn't tell you to eat your vegetables, and although you might not subscribe to everything you were told as a child, mother was certainly right in this instance.

CHAPTER ELEVEN

COENZYME Q_{10}
THE CARDIAC SUPPLEMENT

Our bodies are made up of cells. The cells are the unit of function within the body. Different organs have different cells which work together to perform the necessary function of that organ.

The cells, however, share many common structures one of which is the mitochondria. The mitochondria is the energy producer of the cell. Our cells need energy to function. Without this energy, all the normal functions of the cell cannot occur.

One of the major energy providers in our bodies is adenosine triphosphate (ATP). Coenzyme Q_{10} is an essential chemical for the production of ATP. It was first discovered in 1957 but is still not widely accepted by the medical profession as an important supplement, particularly in relation to cardiac disease. This is despite strong evidence in support of coenzyme Q_{10}.

Heart Failure

There have been 15 randomised trials looking at coenzyme Q_{10} and heart failure. Only one in the 15 trials showed no benefit. All the others showed various benefits from a reduction in symptoms to improved survival. Doses of coenzyme Q_{10} varied between 30 to 200 mgs per day with the average dose being 100 mgs per day. Still coenzyme Q_{10} is not used routinely for heart failure. It has a low side effect profile, an excellent safety record and obviously works.

Angina

There have been five controlled trials of coenzyme Q_{10} in the treatment of angina. All five showed striking improvement for angina. The mode of action is believed to be due to either its ability to improve the efficiency of energy production or by acting as a powerful antioxidant, preventing free radical accumulation.

Heart Surgery

Coronary artery bypass surgery is one of the most common operations performed in the world. The basic principle of this operation is to restore blood flow to a heart that has partial blockages. The body has a series of mechanisms it uses

Some studies have suggested that coenzyme Q_{10} can enhance the effect of vitamin E.

to protect any organ. If the blood supply is impaired due to blockages, the metabolism behind the blockage is slowed down and the local function is reduced.

In the heart, this process is usually referred to as hibernation. When the blood flow is restored, this 'sleeping muscle' does not have enough energy to cope with its new blood supply and, under the stress of the immediate post surgery period, the heart can fail. In a number of studies, coenzyme Q_{10} has been shown to either prevent or significantly improve this scenario. Again, this is not a routine treatment following cardiac surgery.

The interesting finding with coenzyme Q_{10} is that it does not seem to have much effect in the short term. It appears that the most benefit is derived from at least two to three months of vitamin therapy before the coronary artery bypass surgery. Don't expect a huge benefit in under two months of treatment. Also, the sicker the patient, the higher the doses needed. In very sick patients, doses between 300 to 600 mgs per day have been used.

LDL cholesterol oxidisation

LDL cholesterol is the bad cholesterol. It is this stuff that creates the fatty plaques within your arteries. For LDL to create a plaque it must enter the wall of the artery in the oxidised form. Free radicals oxidise the LDL cholesterol. This is precisely how antioxidants work. They prevent this free radical oxidisation by stabilising electrons. LDL cholesterol is protected from oxidisation by vitamin E, which coats the molecule. Vitamin E, therefore, acts as a shield around LDL, protecting it from those free radicals. The problem is, however, that once a free radical attacks vitamin E, it steals an electron from vitamin E (rather than LDL) and this makes vitamin E unstable with the potential of becoming pro–oxidant, therefore a free radical itself.

Although coenzyme Q_{10} has its own antioxidant properties, it is also versatile and can donate some extra electrons back to vitamin E, thus restoring vitamin E to its original antioxidant state. Dr Stocker and his group from Australia showed that a combination of vitamin E and coenzyme Q_{10} was much more effective as an antioxidant combination than vitamin E alone.

The statins and coenzyme Q_{10}

The most powerful cholesterol lowering pills are the statins. Statins are also known as HMG Co–A reductase inhibitors (sorry about this but it is important to develop my point). The Co–A bit stands for coenzyme A. This Co–A is not only important in the production of cholesterol, but also in the production of coenzyme Q_{10}.

Although it is important in many cases to lower cholesterol with the 'statins' (Zocor, Pravachol, Mevacor, Lescol, Vastin, Lipobay or Lipitor), there is now strong evidence that these drugs also lower the level of coenzyme Q_{10} throughout the body.

In some cases there has been impairment in cardiac muscle function (and skeletal muscle function) following the administration of statins, which can be reversed by the subsequent use of coenzyme Q_{10}.

Other benefits of coenzyme Q_{10}

There is also some work to show coenzyme Q_{10} can assist in the lowering of blood pressure. The blood pressure, angina and heart drugs known as beta–blockers have been shown to reduce coenzyme Q_{10} levels. Apart from its use in cardiovascular disease, where I must say I can see no real downside, coenzyme Q_{10} appears promising in other areas.

Cancer

There is limited research into the use of coenzyme Q_{10} in the cancer field. In one study of breast cancer, 32 women were given standard surgical and chemotherapeutic treatment, along with a combination of supplemental antioxidants in high doses including 90 mgs of coenzyme Q_{10} per day. There was a promising response to treatment with no deaths during the study period and no evidence of significant spread of the disease.

I must point out that this was a small non–blinded, non–placebo controlled trial and, although I strongly support the use of nutritional supplementation in many circumstances, I see this as being an addition to standard medical therapy. Standard medical therapy

It is important to discuss your symptoms, your condition and your treatment with your family doctor.

has a proven, scientific track record and has saved many lives. As I continue to emphasise throughout this book – don't ever regard any type of supplementation as a replacement for a healthy lifestyle, appropriate medical assessments and proven medical therapies.

Exercise

I first heard of coenzyme Q_{10} back in the 1980s when a friend of mine told me he was giving it to his greyhounds to enhance their performance. As coenzyme Q_{10} works in the mitochondria, (the energy producing area of the cells) there is some logic to this concept. The muscles are a major energy user in the body and it is possible that supplementing with coenzyme Q_{10} will promote muscle strength and physical performance. One study from Finland in cross–country skiers showed an improvement in physical performance in those given coenzyme Q_{10}.

Summary

Coenzyme Q_{10} can certainly be regarded as the cardiac supplement. I would suggest it be used in conjunction with vitamin E. If you do not have cardiac disease but are concerned about your risk (such as a strong family history or high cholesterol), I would suggest you take:

– Coenzyme Q_{10} 30 to 50 mgs per day
– Vitamin E 400 to 800 IU per day

If you have established cardiac disease, I would suggest 100 mgs per day of coenzyme Q_{10} as a maintenance dose, increasing this to 200 mgs daily during an acute deterioration in your condition.

CHAPTER TWELVE

FATIGUE AND ITS CAUSES

How many people do you know who claim they feel really well? Fatigue is evident in Western society for many and varied reasons. So the next time you are sitting at your desk mid morning, or even worse soon after lunch, and you develop that uncontrollable urge to yawn, and worse still study the inner aspect of your eyelids, don't feel like Robinson Crusoe.

Fatigue is a universal problem that is almost accepted as normal. There's no doubt that almost every individual alive has suffered fatigue for varying periods at some stage in their life. On the one hand fatigue can be a short–lived problem, possibly related to a late night or it can be a chronic disabling condition that ruins your quality of life.

Although there are well recognised causes of fatigue, there is much dispute between traditional medical circles, and those more willing to embrace complementary approaches, regarding the place of nutritional deficiencies in generating fatigue.

According to traditional Western medicine, if you are a normal weight and eat a balanced diet, you cannot possibly be nutritionally deficient. The so–called subtle deficiencies promoted by complementary medicines (especially companies that produce supplements) have no scientific basis and do not exist, according to the traditionalists. However, as I have stated on numerous occasions throughout this book, this is only one position. It is interesting that there are also prominent people in the scientific field who strongly support the antioxidant supplementation position and also believe that people can suffer subtle nutritional deficiencies.

Around 30% of Western society take daily supplements, suggesting that there are either many gullible people out there or they actually do derive some benefit. It is a controversial but distinct possibility that most of us are deficient in one or more of the vitamins, minerals and trace metals, that our bodies need for day to day functioning. We must also recognise that such deficiency is not the only explanation for our fatigue.

Causes of fatigue
Stress

Any physical, mental or emotional stress can cause fatigue. Physical stresses involve the overuse of our bodies in any way, shape or form. This can be with regular, heavy, manual work or excessive exercise. High performance athletes often overtrain, leading to fatigue and susceptibility to recurrent infections.

Stress can be physical, emotional or environmental. It generates free radicals.

Another form of physical stress is environmental. By living in this modern world we subject ourselves to all manner of environmentally generated chemicals. These chemicals can enter our bodies through our lungs, skin or gastrointestinal tract.

Whether it be work, exercise or the environment, the end result is fatigue. All of these stimuli generate enormous amounts of free radicals, so although fatigue is the initial result, long term the risk of the more serious diseases, heart disease and cancer, is a distinct possibility. This is yet another strong reason to consider regular antioxidant supplementation.

Our brain chemicals (also known as neurotransmitters) are depleted during stress (especially mental or emotional). When we suffer these stresses our brain chemicals are rapidly depleted and we feel drained. We rely heavily on many micronutrients especially the B group vitamins to restore these neurotransmitters.

Depression

Whether we suffer the common reactive depression or the more chemical based endogenous depression, a common presentation is fatigue. If life isn't travelling along the way you wrote the script, you will probably feel tired. Say for example, your best friend dies suddenly, the tax department sends you a letter adding a few zeros to your bill or you find out one of your teenagers has developed a hankering for some illegal substance, you will probably feel somewhat overwhelmed by your situation and feel depressed. Depression and fatigue are usually pretty close cousins.

Chemical or endogenous depression occurs when your 'happy chemicals', the catecholamines and serotonin, are knocked for a six for whatever reason and the depression and fatigue are usually more prolonged and profound.

Sleep Apnoea

For all you women who are fortunate enough to share a bed with a possessor of the XY chromosome (the male version of the Homo sapien race), you probably have experienced on occasions or even on a regular basis, the sound of nocturnal vocal chord gurgling – better known as snoring.

As your favourite male (an assumption) drifts into the deeper phases of sleep, the upper airway relaxes along with the rest of the body, plunging the sufferer into a deeply

sonorous (snoring) state and eventually blocking the upper airway. The body then has to make the decision to stay in a deep sleep (which ordinarily rejuvenates the body) but, unfortunately, in this case the airway blocks and the person stops breathing.

If our friendly snorer does not return to a lighter phase of sleep, he (or less often, she) remains with a closed airway and oxygen has difficulty entering the lungs. An event called death quickly ensues unless the individual decides to re–enter a lighter phase of sleep. Therefore, if you wake up in the morning, your body has decided that breathing was a better option than the deepest of sleeps. You then walk around, for most of the day, feeling like a zombie because of lack of quality sleep.

Sleep apnoea can affect your blood pressure.

John Ginnane is 51 years old. Over the last five years, he noticed progressive fatigue and has recently started to fall asleep during meetings. He hasn't stayed awake watching TV for many months as he plunges into a sonorous stupor. Over this time he has had great difficulty controlling his blood pressure. These symptoms were clearly consistent with sleep apnoea. This was confirmed on a sleep study, and appropriate treatment commenced.

The treatment involves a sophisticated nasal mask that pumps positive pressure air into his airway preventing airway collapse. Since using the mask his fatigue has markedly diminished and his blood pressure is controlled.

Menopause

All females experience menopause usually somewhere between 45 to 55 years of age. You may be surprised to know that around 50% of males experience a similar process at around the same time period. In these days of political correctness, it would be remiss of me to discuss menopause without mentioning the male equivalent.

During female menopause or male andropause, the sex

glands (the ovaries and testes respectively) fail, losing the secretion of the female and male hormones. In females, menopause is characterised by loss of menstruation, fatigue, changes in mood, ranging from intermittent sadness to frank depression, hot flushes, loss of libido and aches and pains. In males (apart from the menstruation), the symptoms are exactly the same with inability to achieve an erection thrown in for (not so) good measure. In both females and males, the treatment is appropriate hormone replacement therapy based on each individual's needs.

General Medical Disorders

The final cause of fatigue is a problem with any organ in the body. This can range from any anaemic state to a glandular disorder such as diabetes or a thyroid abnormality. The list could fill a telephone book but with appropriate investigations supervised by a competent doctor, the cause can usually be detected.

With chronic fatigue syndrome (CFS) there is no real consensus as to the true cause of the condition. The general feeling is that it is an accentuated immune response to some form of toxic exposure such as a virus. There are some people who firmly believe that chronic fatigue is due to a subtle combination of nutritional deficiencies. I have seen some people benefit from a combined antioxidant cocktail. Again, whether this is a 'placebo' response or a true benefit is not really possible to assess.

As with most potential treatments in medicine, there is some science for and some against. I always believe it is important to weigh up the risks and side effects of the treatment and its cost, and then allow the educated sufferer to make up their own mind.

Suffice to say, fatigue is a common complaint that almost all but a select few have suffered at some stage during their travels on this wonderful planet.

Do specific antioxidant dose vitamins work for fatigue? Is there a pick–me–up tonic that will improve your energy levels and make you feel less fatigued? The honest answer to this is 'I don't know.'

What I do know is some people do benefit (energy wise that is) from long term use of antioxidant dose vitamins. Others, no matter what antioxidant cocktail you throw at them, will continue to complain of not enough energy.

As with any situation in life, the ultimate decision is yours. If you persistently feel tired, despite thousands of dollars worth of medical investigations and doctor's visits that reassure you you're as fit as a marathon runner, then I believe an antioxidant dose vitamins cocktail is worth a try, at least for a few months. My suggestion for this daily cocktail is:

1. Multi–B with folic acid (at least 400 mcgs)
2. Bioflavonoid extract for example grapeseed or pinebark derivative
3. Spirulina (a super food usually derived from algae)
4. Vitamin E 500 IU, vitamin C 1,000 mgs and coenzyme Q_{10} 50 mgs
5. Herbal supplements such as gingko biloba

CHAPTER THIRTEEN

COLDS AND FLU

Don't you hate it when someone proudly announces, 'I never get sick, I haven't had a virus for 20 years'. This statement is made to not so subtly suggest that the person's body, and especially their immune system, is really much better than everyone who is susceptible to illness.

Well, if it is true that this particular human being hasn't had a virus for 20 years, then I would have thought it was obvious that they had a pretty efficient immune system, or they were so brain dead they didn't realise they were sick!

Does this mean they have healthier bodies that are less prone to the diseases that count, like our free radical induced enemies, heart disease and cancer? Of course not. It just means that when it comes to common viruses that cause things like a sore throat, runny nose, aches and pains, fevers or diarrhoea and vomiting, each of us reacts differently. If you expose a community to any virus (depending on the strength or virulence of that virus) to cause mischief, usually only a minority of clinical cases will occur. Some overwhelming viruses like influenza may cause problems in over 50% of an affected community, but most viruses will affect a much lesser number.

There are many reasons why only certain people are affected and infected with a particular virus. If a person has had exposure to that virus or a similar virus in the past, the immune system will have developed antibodies and memory cells specific to killing that virus.

When someone is stressed or run down for any reason, their immune system is also not working properly. Most of us have experienced that viral illness, right smack in the middle of a period in our life when we were overworked or had big stresses at home or too may late nights.

The younger we are, the more susceptible we are to viruses. This is due to an immature immune system. The longer we live, the more time we have to be exposed to the vast array of viruses, bacteria and other bugs that share our living space. Also, during our growing years, up to early to mid adulthood, we are often exposed to preschool, school and working environments that have large populations. It only takes one person with the infection to donate this to others. Viruses can travel faster from person to person than gossip.

One of the big misconceptions in respect to viral illnesses is influenza. Influenza is a specific virus that almost always occurs in epidemics. Over the past century there were quite a few lethal epidemics that wiped out many members of the infected population. It is for this infection that the fluvax or 'flu shot' is given. There are many people in society who oppose vaccination. I am certainly not going to engage in a

"On completing her historic flight, in flew..."

debate on the pros and cons of this subject. Suffice to say, if you do have a 'flu shot', don't expect it will prevent you from developing mild viral illnesses, because it won't. It will, either prevent or in some cases lessen the severity of influenza.

The flu vaccination is recommended for older people, people with chronic illnesses or health workers with a large population exposure. I know, personally, in the years I have neglected or forgotten to have the fluvax I developed influenza and was very ill for over a week.

Some people who have the vaccination claim it gives them the flu. This is also a misconception. It may precipitate similar, though less severe, symptoms than the flu itself but it definitely does not cause the infection.

Excessive use of antibiotics leads to antibiotic resistance.

How do you know you've contracted influenza? Firstly many of your family, friends and associates are also sick. Secondly, you usually have the typical symptoms. These are feeling like you're about to depart this mortal coil, often very high fevers, muscle aches and pains, inability to stand up, sore throat, coughing and any other number of nasty symptoms that nature cares to create.

Any combination of symptoms, as just mentioned, can either represent influenza or may just be due to a non–specific virus. As I have mentioned, the 'flu shot' will not prevent these non–specific viruses.

Antibiotics and influenza

So, after a day or two of suffering these symptoms you decide to visit your friendly family physician to be prescribed some proper treatment for this disabling condition. The bad news is that it doesn't matter whether you have full blown influenza or a non–specific virus, there is no antibiotic known that will help.

In fact, if your doctor offers you an antibiotic, he or she is doing the wrong thing. Antibiotics kill bacteria not viruses. Antibiotics also kill all your normal bacteria. So when you take your prescribed medication, you are also wiping out your normal, friendly bacteria that help you fight a virus. Therefore, when you have a viral illness, it is harder to beat when you're on an antibiotic.

Excessive use of antibiotics leads to antibiotic resistance. This problem usually affects the people who need it the least: the elderly, those with chronic illness or are immunocompromised such as cancer sufferers, HIV victims and others suffering immune disorders.

'Superbugs' become resistant to many and in some very scary cases, all antibiotics. The infected person can then develop illness involving:

◆ Blood, for example septicaemia
◆ Lungs, for example pneumonia
◆ Bladder, for example pyelonephritis
◆ Skin, for example golden staph
◆ Infected wounds

Only very heavy doses of powerful antibiotics will make a dent in these 'superbugs'. The death rate amongst people who become afflicted with these monsters is very high.

What to do when you get the flu

Therefore, the next time you think it is important to pressure your doctor into a course of antibiotics to treat your virus, think again. What can you do if you feel a viral illness of any description coming on? My suggestions for coping include:

◆ Rest
◆ Vitamin C 2 gms per day
◆ Echinacea
◆ Garlic
◆ Zinc

Rest

Continuing your normal activities (especially if they are busy and stressful) can keep your immune function at low ebb. So, get yourself on that 'healing lounge' and forget about life for a while.

Vitamin C

Have plenty of citrus fruits and supplement with vitamin C to help strengthen your immune system. I suggest around 2 gms per day, during colds and flu.

Echinacea

This wonderful herb has specific anti–viral properties and is very useful for common respiratory tract viruses. The only downside suggested is that echinacea should be used cautiously with asthmatics. I have personally found, as I am prone to recurrent sore throats and hoarse voice in my job as a doctor and professional speaker, that echinacea has been an effective agent. It has

Gentle exercise boosts the immune system. Intensive exercise depresses the immune system.

helped me through many a consultation and lecture when I thought I would lose my voice.

Garlic

Garlic either as a tasty (though at times socially inhibiting) food, or as a non–odour supplement, has been shown to have immune stimulating properties. Garlic is also a natural blood thinner so it is useful to assist those with circulation problems. There have been suggestions over the past thirty years that garlic lowers the cholesterol. In a carefully designed study performed by Professor Leon Simons at St Vincent's Hospital in Sydney, there was no significant reduction in cholesterol in those taking garlic supplements.

Zinc

It is now accepted, especially in children, that zinc reduces the infection rate and the severity of respiratory illnesses, including pneumonia. The dose of zinc (for adults usually as lozenges) is 10 mgs 3 to 5 times per day.

CHAPTER FOURTEEN

THE YOUNG AND THE OLD
SPECIAL CIRCUMSTANCES

Athletes

How often do you hear of high performance athletes dropping dead from heart disease prematurely? How many develop cancer for no obvious reason? These strange and not too infrequent tragic occurrences prompted Dr Kenneth Cooper, the pioneer of the aerobics craze in the 1970s, to completely re–evaluate his position on the practice of excessive exercise.

Basically Cooper admitted his initial advice and position needed to be reconsidered and in his later book, *The Antioxidant Revolution*, he expounds the benefits of low impact exercise and the consumption of antioxidant dose vitamins.

So what is the problem with exercise? We all know that without exercise we start to assume the proportions of creatures members of Greenpeace keep trying to drag off their beach towel and push back into the ocean!. It gets back to the age old principle – it's all about balance. Too little is bad but so is too much.

Excessive weight, from a sedentary lifestyle, causes all sorts of problems. Overweight people develop all types of illnesses,

ranging from high blood pressure to diabetes, gallstones and arthritis. Heart disease and common cancers are also much more common in the obese.

At the other end of the spectrum high performance athletes usually have little or no body fat and don't appear to have the common obesity related diseases. However, they do not appear to live much longer than the obese.

Cooper is not alone in presenting the theory that excessive exercise damages the muscles, and produces a marked increase in free radical production. These free radicals then damage LDL cholesterol, the blood vessel wall and also DNA, setting the athlete up for heart disease or cancer.

I am not suggesting that anyone who has played some high level competitive sport, or has competed in marathons, should book the early train to Grim Reaper City, but I am suggesting that people who do perform this high

Sweating results in the loss of the trace elements iron and zinc.

level activity should consider the following point. Exercise only protects you for the time you are exercising. Within around six weeks of stopping exercise, the benefits wear off.

I don't know how many patients I have seen with significant heart problems making comments to me like, 'I can't possibly have a problem, I was an Olympic rower 20 years ago!'

Steve is 45 years old. He was an Olympic swimmer and still swims two kilometres three to four times per week. He attended my clinic for a high speed CT scan of his coronary arteries. He is thin with an athletic body but has a high cholesterol level. He was shocked when his result was 250 (in the moderate range for coronary calcium). He did not take antioxidants up to that point, but fortunately the fat in his arteries had not as yet caused him problems. With appropriate management, I believe we will be able to prevent Steve from having an acute coronary episode in the future.

I do, however, believe it was Steve's high level activity that has contributed to the early fat build up in his arteries. It is my recommendation for athletes that they consume a daily combination of:

1. Vitamin E 800 to 1,000 IU
2. Vitamin C 1,000 mgs
3. Beta–carotene 12 mgs
4. Multi–B with folic acid
5. Coenzyme Q_{10} 50 mgs

Pregnancy

The issue of supplements in pregnancy is a difficult one. Many conservative medical scientists and practitioners start to trot out the hackneyed argument that taking unnatural substances into the body during pregnancy can cause all types of problems from cleft palates to severe heart abnormalities. I would like to present an alternative argument, combined with a strong element of caution. It is likely that many in Western society, although overfed with the macronutrients fat, protein and carbohydrates, have subtle deficiencies of micronutrients. This argument has been strengthened in the case of pregnancy where there is a definite association between low levels of folic acid and neural tube defects, which can produce the condition spina bifida. I believe it causes a growing foetus much more harm to be deficient in an essential micronutrient than to have an abundance.

One of the other issues that seems to be missed is the fact that a woman should create an environment as ideal as possible for her baby to be conceived. Many women are not trying to become pregnant and therefore do not know they are pregnant until around eight weeks after the event. Any harmful behaviour such as poor nutrition, cigarette smoking, excessive alcohol consumption, drug abuse or chronic stress, can affect the baby in its crucial early phase of growth.

The effects of helpful nutrients or harmful toxins are more profound during the first few months of growth rather than the last two–thirds of pregnancy.

The main micronutrient in supplemental doses shown to cause harm in pregnancy is vitamin A. One study showed a five times higher risk for birth defects in the babies of mothers who consumed greater than 10,000 IU of vitamin A per day. Another study looking at the same subject showed no difference in birth defect rates even up to doses of 25,000 IU.

In the first study, the risk appeared to be greatest in the earlier phases of pregnancy. Vitamin A is probably not a major problem, but I certainly would not take this risk. I would strongly suggest that a woman wanting to become pregnant should follow these guidelines:

1. Most importantly, follow the principles of healthy nutrition, consuming mainly the Mediterranean diet concentrating on plenty of fruits and vegetables.
2. Do not smoke
3. Regular gentle exercise
4. Keep your alcohol down to at most one to two glasses per day (if at all during this important time)
5. Try to minimise stress in your life

In addition to this, daily intake of supplements containing:

- Folic acid 400 mcg
- Iron – 30 mgs
- Multi–B 25 to 50 mgs
- Vitamin C 500 mgs and vitamin E 250 mgs
- Calcium 1,000 mgs, magnesium 100 mgs and zinc 15 mgs

Children

I am often asked, should children be taking antioxidant dose vitamins? Although I believe a growing body needs a significant amount of vitamins, I am not sure the long term benefits justify the cost. Children are at very low risk for cancer and heart disease and therefore you are treating a large group of the population with supplements to prevent a

During pregnancy a woman's energy requirements increase by 20%.

very small incidence of disease. My usual recommendation is for people to start supplementing around the age of 35 years.

I must also add, if your children are anything like mine, they tend to remember to raid the fridge and cupboards regularly, but easily forget to take their multivitamins.

For those parents who are truly concerned their children have an inadequate diet, there are now many excellent vitamins (often tasty, chewable form or in tasty bars) that will give children the additional micronutrients they lack in their diets.

Unfortunately, many of the foods children are attracted to contain large amounts of saturated fats and refined sugars. Be a mother and tell them to eat their fruit and vegetables.

Aging

As we age, we probably require less macronutrients because our activity is somewhat reduced. We still require the same amounts of micronutrients but probably more in antioxidant doses. The longer we live, the longer our exposure to free radicals. That is precisely why the older we are, the more prone we are to free radical disease such as heart disease and cancer.

This is why I believe it is even more vital for those over the age of 55 (I am certainly not classing this as old) to be very diligent in regard to their antioxidant and micronutrient intake. I recommend a daily supplement intake that includes:

1. Ginko biloba
2. Coenzyme Q_{10} 50 to 100 mgs
3. Vitamin E 400 to 800 IU and vitamin C 1,000 mgs
4. Beta–carotene 6 to 12 mgs
5. Multi–B with folic acid 400 mcg

CHAPTER FIFTEEN

CONCLUSION

Antioxidant dose vitamins are not miracle cures. In fact, the so called miracle cures do not exist. Coronary artery bypass grafting does not cure heart disease and is, in reality, a temporary procedure until you can get your life in order.

Basically, until you've corrected the cause of whatever disease befalls you, it will recur after a certain time period, despite the best efforts of the surgeon or some other physician. The responsibility is yours and yours alone. Your doctor will give you all the appropriate advice you need, but he or she can't force you to follow that advice.

If you are at low or high risk for disease, lifestyle modifications and adjustments are the most important part of your health management plan. If you suffer an acute event such as a heart attack, a major bleed, a severe infection or present with some form of cancer, the best place for you is in a hospital having medical or surgical therapy. Once the acute event has settled, the best long term management is to continue your medical treatment along with lifestyle modification and appropriate supplementation.

Your lifelong management on a day to day, month by month, year by year and decade by decade basis is the most vital. To reiterate, the five point way to optimum health is:

1. Diet
2. Exercise and movement
3. Not smoking
4. Moderate correct alcohol intake
5. Stress management

These lifestyle factors are designed to help you find an optimum balance. They will give you the best chance of fighting the free radical attacks on your body. This will help prevent degenerative diseases such as heart disease, cancer, diabetes and osteoporosis.

You also need to have regular, accurate medical assessments. Many people have poor genetics that predispose them to premature diseases. Appropriate medical assessments can detect these conditions early and avoid the strong possibility of serious illness.

Life is a joy. It is a privilege to be alive and to savour all that our world offers. Part of that privilege is the vehicle we have been given to carry us through our journey. That vehicle needs to be treated with the utmost care and respect. If you choose to live life to the fullest with quality and quantity, follow my five point plan and I can promise you this is your highway to health.

Strategy? No, they're trying to remember lunch.

GLOSSARY OF TERMS

amino acid: Amino acids join together to make up proteins. There are eight amino acids that cannot be synthesised in our bodies and must be obtained from diet.

angina pectoris: Chest pain with exertion or stress caused by insufficient blood supply to the heart muscle.

angiogram: A diagram of the blood vessels of the heart created after the injection of dye.

antioxidant: Any substance that destroys oxidising agents. Free radical scavengers are antioxidants. Examples of antioxidants are vitamins C and E, beta-carotene and coenzyme Q_{10}.

atheroma: Fatty deposits in blood vessels that may eventually cause narrowing and restriction of blood supply. They consist of oxidised lipids and cholesterol, collagen, platelets, and white blood cell by-products.

atherosclerosis: The progressive deposition of fat and eventually calcium within the blood vessel wall. This is the usual predisposing cause of heart attack, angina and sudden cardiac death.

carcinogen: A chemical substance that when introduced into the body has the potential to cause cancer.

cardiovascular disease: Disease of the heart and circulation system which results in heart attacks and strokes.

cholesterol: A sterol found in all animals and an essential component of cell membranes. LDL (bad) cholesterol can form fatty deposits and HDL (good) cholesterol can discourage these same formations.

coronary heart disease: Condition caused by disease of the arteries carrying blood to the heart, usually due to atherosclerosis.

DNA: DNA makes up the genetic material in a cell and is inherited. DNA plays an important role in the control of health and disease.

endothelial cells: The single layer of cells that line the interior of blood vessels, the heart and the lymph vessels.

enzyme: An enzyme is a protein that is a catalyst. It speeds up chemical processes within the body.

epidemiology: The study of the distribution of disease where some characteristic of a large group of apparently healthy people is measured, such as the dietary intake of vitamin E. Taken from the word epidemic which affects a large group of people

epithelial cells: A single layer of cells covering a surface and performing a protective role, such as the skin.

free radical: A free radical is any atom or molecule having one or more unpaired electrons. They react inside us constantly damaging cells, HDL cholesterol and DNA. Antioxidants fight them.

gene: A gene is the basic hereditary unit responsible for the synthesis of a protein and is associated with DNA.

glutathione: A sulphur-containing tripeptide made up of one molecule each of the amino acids glutamine, glycine, and cysteine. It is one of the most important antioxidants in our bodies, especially in the lungs and gastrointestinal tract. hormone: Is a chemical produced in minute quantities by an endocrine gland and moved around the body to control the activity of organs and other glands.

hypertension: An elevation of the blood pressure which can indicate coronary heart disease.

lipid: Lipid is the biological term for a fat, and is any substance containing a fatty acid.

metabolism: The chemical reactions occurring within an organism which can be fast or slow. It includes the breaking down of complex organic compounds to simple ones.

micronutrient: A vitamin,mineral or trace element that we must obtain from our diet to maintain health.

mutation: A change in DNA that alters the information stored. Mutations form the basis of evolutionary change.

They are normally infrequent, but the rate can be increased by exposing cells to free radicals. If a mutation is malignant the affecting agent is called a carcinogen.

omega-3 fatty acids: The omega-3 fatty acids are found in fish oils, linseed, canola, and soya bean. The other important family of polyunsaturated fatty acids is the omega-6 fatty acids.

oxidation: Addition of oxygen to an atom or molecule, or removal of an electron from an atom or molecule. Oxidation affects reactions such as the browning of an apple or the souring of wine on exposure to oxygen, or the creation of rust. Antioxidants prevent oxidation.

pathology: The study of disease, especially the changes in tissue and organs as a result of disease.

polyunsaturated fatty acid: A fatty acid with two or more double unsaturated bonds such as those found in safflower oil and margarines.

standard drink: A standard alcoholic drink contains 10 gms of alcohol.

trans-fatty acids: Trans-fatty acids are formed during hydrogenation of fatty acids in the production of some margarines and shortbreads. Consumption of trans-fatty acids has increased dramatically in the 20th century, and is now about 10% to 15% of our fat intake. These synthetic fatty acids are inflammatory and could be involved in allergic conditions and a range of degenerative diseases.

triglyceride: A compound formed between one molecule of glycerol and three fatty acid molecules. Most fats are triglycerides or compounds of glycerol and fatty acids.

vascular: Concerning vessels that carry blood around the body.

vitamin: Substances found in many foodstuffs and supplements. Essential for the maintenance of life. Lack of vitamins can result in a deficiency disease and moderate amounts are necessary to achieve antioxidant levels.